I0423548

PROTESTS AND RIOTS

Challenging Inept Governance

by John Tomikel

ISBN 978-1505223965

ISBN 15052233962

It is the duty of all who wish justice to protest against injustice and the most obvious place to start is with discriminatory legislation. When asked why he was in prison, Thoreau asked, "and why are you out there?"

For Bruce Boland, long-time antagonist and friend.

Democracy is not a spectator sport.

I THE SET UP

Injustice demands protest. The ballot box has proven to be an object of manipulation. People no longer trust the government that seems to be divided on every issue. Senator Toomey of Pennsylvania said his co-sponsored gun bill would have passed Congress but his Republican Party didn't want to give President Obama any positive accomplishments while he was in office.

The far right activists have pretty much succeeded in convincing a large number of citizens that the government is the enemy of the people. They have succeeded in demonizing President Obama to the point of low popularity. They became proficient at demonizing by working on Speaker of the House Nancy Pelosi. These extremists do not seem to take responsibility for their followers gunning down policemen in restaurants and other habitats.

Is there some justification for police shooting unarmed civilians, even though they have shown hostility? How should we respond to indignities?

Recent public protests have ended in huge destruction of property and the loss of some life. The shooting of a black man in Missouri by a white policeman was an excuse for civil disobedience which was marked by criminal action. It seemed to be a good chance to pick up a free case of beer and a new TV. Never mind due process. But, perhaps the situation did call for wide-spread protest and discussion.

Historically, revolutions have been a response to the inability of citizens to engage in the decision making processes of their government. It is obvious that we cannot change democratic ideals by appealing to our legislators so we must change the decision making process by other means, mainly civil disobedience. We must consider what form of civil disobedience is best engaged to correct an injustice, real or perceived.

In encouraging civil disobedience we must do it on a rational basis and try to eliminate emotional aspects of the situation in question.

We can try to avoid emotional entanglements with animal rights, abortion, gay marriage, euthanasia and such topics. Our revolution should be concerned with access to the legislative process such as open referendum and sunshine laws, which in many places exist in name only. A quick run-down on some national situations would be helpful in this discussion. My own prejudices will be obvious.

In the last thirty years the Congress of the United States has catered to the interests of the rich and privileged over the interests of the ordinary citizens of the country. The gap between the rich and the poor started to widen under the Reagan administration and has continued to widen to the present day. Meanwhile the national debt continues to increase at alarming rates. Again we must go back to the Reagan administration where the debt level was increased eleven times. When Reagan left office he left the country with the biggest national debt in the history of the country. His legacy, the debt, was greater than all the presidents combined that served before him.

Somehow Reagan captured the fancy of right wing activists and they have transformed him into something greater than human. In their adulation, any negative facet of reality concerning him is ignored. It is difficult to have a realistic dialogue with these admirers since with them the legacy of Reagan has passed from history to mythology and folklore.

Reagan was a pleasant person who came up with a lot of bumper sticker sayings that are still quoted today. However, his actions speak louder than words and in order to understand what he did to the country one has to throw all loyalty aside. His removal on constraints over the Savings and Loan organizations cost the taxpayers millions of dollars, if not billions.

The policies of Reagan are not entirely to blame for the financial and social mess we are in since his policies have been intensified by those who came after him. One of his famous remarks, "Deficits don't matter" was geared toward winning a second term and not a realistic appraisal of the condition of the country.

Of the recent presidents I liked George Bush The First probably more than the others. He was, in my opinion the most qualified person to be president since Thomas Jefferson. When George Bush I had a chance to amend some of the deficit mentally of the legislators, he missed the opportunity. He further lost credibility in world opinion when he refused to acknowledge America's role in the creation of greenhouse gases and our responsibility toward that situation. His main interest was to protect America's industrial base, which is a noble position if we look at it from our own economic survival. If this protection was filtered down to the average citizen it would have been commendable. However, the rich continued to get richer and the poor continued to increase in numbers.

President Clinton began to get the budget under control and when he left office he left a budget surplus but the country was still holder of a massive debt. When Clinton initiated several trade agreements he effectively cut American jobs and sent them to other countries. His role in this and the unemployment of Americans cannot be ignored. It might be argued that creating jobs in Mexico slowed down illegal crossing of our border by Mexicans.

The election of George Bush II and his cohort Dick Cheney was a disaster for America. Their tax breaks for the rich broke the bank. The Supreme Court involvement in the election of Bush II was a disgrace to our country. The supporters of Bush II were the champions of state's rights until their interests were jeopardized and so brought in their (not the people's) Supreme Court to back them up.

Cheney's arrogant thug like influence over Bush II in the early years of their administration led us into two useless, financially expensive and morally expensive wars. The dictator of Iraq was displaced at the cost of over four thousand American lives and at least a hundred thousand innocent civilian lives of Iraq. The invasion of Iraq was supposedly not about oil, but a concern for human survival since the dictator allegedly had weapons of mass destruction. Cheney often used the phrase, "We have it on good authority" and his authoritative source, more often than not, proved to be wrong. Where was Congress at this time? They were busy running for re-election.

Lori Montgomery, writing in the Washington Post in July 2011, pretty much summed up the Bush II legacy. When Bush came into office with a surplus it was assumed that he would pay back most of the debt of the country. Rather than use the surplus to pay down the debt or fix Social Security he maneuvered two massive tax cuts. Bush and Congress then entered into two wars at the initial cost of $1.3 trillion. He then went on to spend $272 billion on Medicare prescription benefits as well as expanding defense and domestic spending. He billed himself as a "compassionate conservative" "Bush II policies accounts for $7 trillion dollars of the present national debt."

President Barack Obama has desperately tried to clean up the mess of the former administration. He appears to be adding to the mess. His $719 billion stimulus program was simply expenditure. At this writing his programs have added $1.7 trillion more to the national dept. The opposition to him does not seem to be on rational grounds but rather some sort of emotional odyssey. The opposition is not concentrating on the interests of the country but seems to have as it's goal "get Obama" at all costs. None of the actors in this drama want to seriously address the high unemployment and the financial decline of the country. Their words have hollow meaning and their pious expressions are false.

When a person making over eleven million dollars a year pays no income tax and Congress does not address this situation then we have only one recourse and that is to somehow change the nature of our government, since we seem to be unable to change the nature of our legislators. The usual statement, by those in charge, is that we should change the situation at the ballot box. However, psychological and pathological actions are at work in the election process and those in charge know it and how to take advantage of it. Not only money is involved in elections but a demoralizing plethora of recrimination and ill will. No action is too debasing when winning an election is at stake. One of our present great statesman, John McCain, was so demonized in his primary bid against Bush II the country's fantasy of "high-standard" morality was mocked.

We need a revolution in this country, not a revolution to overthrow the government, but a revolution to change how the country and the legislators that make the laws think. There are laws and practices that are unfair and most legislators know them for what they are. They seem to want to keep their seats at the cost of their own moral fiber.

One such law governing the political contributions to a candidate could easily be corrected and that is for the candidate to disclose his contributors, every cent countable and every name is given. That way, we can evaluate and openly discuss the connection between contributors and legislation. No registered candidate should be allowed to accept an anonymous contribution. Any anonymous contribution should be channeled to the Federal Election Fund connected to the 1040 form.

The Constitution of the United States is indeed one of the great documents of world history. Its checks and balances are a sound principle. However, under Bush II and his henchman Cheney the Executive usurped more power than the "checks and balances" should tolerate. It was difficult to identify who was president and who was vice president. Comedians and cartoonists emphasized this situation many times. President Obama has been accused of violating the constitution. If this is so, why don't those who make this claim initiate impeachment. It seems they would rather work with innuendo than facts.

The Supreme Court does not seem to be the unbiased body that it was intended to be. Their many recent decisions have put the interests of the privileged before those of the country. Case in point, the discrimination suit against Walmart.

But the question is how do you get people interested in something as cerebral as the tax code, bureaucratic waste, monetary influence, and pork legislation? "I will vote for your pork if you vote for mine." Who is willing to march on Washington to get financial disclosure information laws amended? Not enough to make an impact. Yet this is vital to understanding the moral consciousness of our legislators. They should be doing this without our prodding.

In the following discussion I will try to give the reader some indication of revolutionary methods and thinking that could be employed to change the course of our government.

There are several friends of mine who have strong opinions on these matters, many personally conflicting, whom I shall quote. Rather than name them individually I will lump them into one character whom I shall call Fred. These quotes are from real people that I know personally. So it is possible that Fred will have conflicting views but he is a tool with which I can give a slant to an opinion. For instance, Fred is opposed to social security but he collects it. He was in favor of the Bush II proposal of privatizing social security. When his other retirement income was hit hard by the drop in stock market values he didn't waver in his support of privatizing social security. He never wavered in his vote of straight Republican, even though it was not in his best financial interests to do so. He refuses to accept the fact that the greatest tax increase in the history of the country at that time was under President Reagan.

Survival in Society

A study of animal life reveals certain truths that pertain to humans since we are basically a part of the animal world. Animals reproduce at a rate higher than the environment can support. For instance, a clam will produce two million viable offspring. When the clam larva hatch they must compete with each other for the available food. They must also compete with other species for the same food. Also, they become food for other species. As a result, only two of the hatched larva will make it to adulthood and be able to reproduce. To describe this the term "survival of the fittest" is often used since it is assumed those that survived were best fit for survival.

Humans also reproduce more offspring than the environment can support. There is competition for the resources of the environment and those who garner the most of these resources are the people who will survive the best in the environment. The major other group of animals competing for the same food are insects, but we compete for the food that insects don't get.

By banding together with groups we have a better chance to survive as an individual. The group is more capable of protecting an area of the environment better than an individual. The strongest and cleverest people of the group usually acquire leadership positions within the group and make the decisions for the group.

The leaders of the group usually make certain that they are the first in line when the benefits of the environment are distributed. They remain in leadership by exercising power over the rest of the group.

Like the young clams we are all in competition for the benefits derived from the environment. If we are successful we are able to pass our successful genes on to our progeny who with these attributes will also be successful in obtaining the benefits of the environment.

Conflict between groups of people are the result of a group wanting to change the division of environmental resources and, of course, get more of it for themselves. Those who are best adapted to the environment, socially as well as physically, will be the best at survival.

So when we look inside a given area such as a country we see the same mechanisms at work. Groups band together to insure the survival of the group and individuals within the group..

Inside the group there is competition for survival at an optimum level which can be called life style. It boils down to a dog-eat-dog world. What is reality is that your best friend is in competition with you and more often than not would, as they say, throw you under the bus rather than sacrifice his own level of survival.

So we can look upon the dominant group as having the best portion of the resources that the environment can provide. They share this within the group to some extent. The lowest member of the group gets the least, but he still has more of the resources than a member of a competing minority group.

In order to stay in power the group must be strong or make concessions to other groups or individuals that also have power.

Our political system is geared to alliances and confederations of groups. Thus white well- heeled men become Republicans and non-white less heeled men become Democrats. There is, of course, overlapping in these stereotypes.

In order to stay in power the political party must make concessions to groups that have economic power and who can buy the votes or to groups large enough in number to sway an election. There are many methods that can be used to insure an election victory and these are generally related to the resources which is translated for convenience into money.

When concessions to some groups are so large that it deprives a large number of individuals the basic necessities of life then the large number of individuals must band together to retrieve the concessions from the people with power. If these disgruntled people are large in number and their will is strong then they can wrest the power from the other group and get a better share of the resources which will insure their own survival. In a large group, leadership is important. In a small group, understanding the objective might be enough to achieve results.

In the conflict over resources a favorite and successful tactic of the small group in power is to divide the larger group into smaller divisions. By doing so, the small group in power, becomes formidable since it can then combat these smaller divisions one at a time. After demolishing the air traffic controller unions they can then turn their attention to the auto workers and tell them the same thing will happen to them if they don't comply. By taking on the smaller divisions first they have more ammunition for taking on the larger divisions when the time comes for them to do so.

We have to consider individual actions as a facet of evolution. We are programmed with an instinct for survival and when we look at actions of individuals in that context it make more sense even though we don't agree with the actions.

When a riot occurs the mob usually moves as a unit from one type of action to another. The actions may be described as chaotic or anarchist, and the mob designated as unorganized. The mob may appear chaotic as a whole but the individual within that mob is following his instinct for survival. He knows exactly the nature of his philosophy concerning his actions, even though he doesn't think in those terms. This is also assuming that the actor is not on some mind altering substances.

Smashing and burning objects is a method of depriving someone else of objects that represent survival and thus diminishes the owners ability to survive by some minor increment. Perhaps the rioter decides to steal a television set. The television represents wealth which represents an increment of survival. So by taking the television set the rioter moves up a little on the survival ladder. He can transfer the TV set into food and clothing if he so wishes, which are basic to survival.

When a Mexican illegally crosses the U.S. Border he, of course, is seeking a better life. Since we don't shoot illegals at the border his chances of getting this better life are pretty good. If he is caught and returned to Mexico he can always move over a couple of miles and try again. It is survival and I'm sure everyone recognizes it as such.

How about documenting the illegals when they are apprehended and the second time coming across and captured execute them? Perhaps tattooing them the first time to make the second recognition easier. But this is inhumane and we are noted for our humanity.

Even legal immigration presents a problem. The immigrants are healthy, which is a requirement for immigration, and have a sponsor. Once here, they work on getting the rest of the family here. The immigrant misses his family and wishes they were with him. Of course, the immigrant going back to the family he misses is not an option for him.

When a legal, or illegal, immigrant comes into this country he uses a certain amount of resources for his survival. As he consumes these resources it diminishes the amount of resources we have for our own survival. As a result, his survival is enhanced by an increment and our survival is diminished by an increment. That's one way to look at it.

Israel Protest 2011

Israel July 2011 – An ongoing protest got its start when around 300 thousand people took to the streets in Tel Aviv. Many of them set up tents with the idea of hanging on and continuing the protest once the initial protest was over. Leaders of the protest said they wanted to reduce the cost of housing as well as the cost of food and child care since in many cases both parents were working to make ends meet. The protesters were emboldened by the successful protesters in other parts of the Middle East.

Israel is fairly prosperous when all is considered. Their economic growth has averaged five percent annually in the last eight years. Protesters say this hasn't filtered down to the common people.

Apparently the Prime Minister, Ben Natanyaho thinks the government can do something about the problem since he has promised to "reassess his priorities and make housing more affordable."

Protesting is a successful enterprise in Israel since the government is very sensitive to the pulse of the people. In September 2010, the main airport of Tel Aviv was closed when union officials called a strike after pension talks collapsed.

The main thrust of the strike was that the pension fund would be secure and not used for other purposes, an action which appeared to be in progress. The complaint or fear is similar to that in the United States where monies generated for Social Security and Medicare have been manipulated and used for other purposes.

What made the airport strike effective was its timing and correlation with the holy days of Rosh Hashanah and Yom Kippur.

If we are to consider successful revolution as a progressive act then we should consider those revolutions that have changed the government system in the land in which they occurred.

It seems in every country there are people who are frustrated by the regime under which they live. It is only natural that they should wish to change the nature of that regime. When the numbers of those who are discontented rise to a critical level then the country is ready for revolution.

The government that is the recipient of the revolt has several options, among them (1) it can put down the revolt by military means, (2) it can change the conditions of the country that is the focus of the revolt, and (3) they could resign and let some other group take over the leadership of the country. Generally when a government resigns there is no shortage of groups or individuals willing to take its place.

When a government loses control of its country usually anarchy results unless one group is in place ready to take over the obligations of government. The situation of anarchy often follows the fall of a government and the first duty of the new government is to restore order. This often takes repressive measures. Once control has been established the repressive measure must be removed or else the new government will become the target of a new revolution.

Since state (countries) borders have been pretty much established and accepted by most countries of the world it seems unlikely that an invasion of one country by another will be tolerated in today's world. The major changes that will take place in the future will be nations breaking away from states or divisions of countries along cultural lines. It is also possible that areas such as North Korea and South Korea will merge into one national unit.

In the United States our revolution must be an internal revolution which will lead to a better life for the majority of our citizens who are willing to work. Those not willing to work will have to accept a lower economic status and be content with a less consuming life style than those capable and willing to work.

The government has an obligation to see that work is available to the masses. It is disgraceful that the best jobs in this country, for the average person, are those within the government. A sizable segment of the population decries socialism but yet they want the benefits of employment with the federal or state government.

Our system of taxation concerning profits made by foreign investment needs drastically overhauled. If some foreign investor wishes to be a citizen of this country then he should pay taxes on his income regardless of where that income was obtained.

Years ago I went to purchase a stove at a Sears store. I asked the clerk if it was made in America. He said in a pontifical voice that it was made by Sears workers in a Sears factory in Taiwan. He said it as if a Sears factory in Taiwan was somehow good for America. We get cheaper goods from foreign countries but they will not be purchased when we no longer have personal income with which to do so. As our productive industries continues to decline, so will our income and eventually the two will be the destruction of American society as we know it.

II SIGNIFICANT REVOLUTIONS

Enlightenment

To understand the need for revolution we should know the origin of modern human rights thinking and avocation. The era of free thinking and intellectual freedom has been called The Age of Enlightenment. Thomas Paine called it The Age of Reason. It was a combination of published thoughts by philosophers in Europe over a time span of more than a hundred years. It took time for the word to spread. The French Revolution is considered the culmination of this thinking. Historical enlightenment promoted intellectual exchange of ideas, opposed intolerance and exposed abuses in church and state.

Enlightenment advocated reason as a means to establish an authoritative system of government, religion and ethics. This would allow humans to obtain objective truth about reality. Enlightenment thinkers argued that reason could free humankind from superstition and religious authoritarianism that had brought suffering and death to millions in religious wars. The wide availability of this thinking and knowledge was made possible through the Enlightenment cause of educating the human race.

The center of the Enlightenment was France where it was the center of conversation in all the intellectual circles. The culmination of these discussions was the publication in 1751 of the thirty two volume *Encyclopedie* edited by Denis Diderot. It had the published philosophies of most all the thinkers in previous history, especially those of that present day. It sold over 25,000 copies, more than half of them outside of France.

The new intellectual forces spread to urban centers across Europe, notably England, Scotland, the German states, the Netherlands, Russia, Italy, Austria, and Spain, then jumped the Atlantic into the European colonies, where it influenced Benjamin Franklin and Thomas Jefferson, among many others and played a role in the American Revolution. Its political ideals influenced the American

Declaration of Independence, the United States Bill of Rights, the French Declaration of the Rights of Man and the Citizen and the Polish-Lithuanian Constitution of May 3, 1791.

The intellectual leaders of the Enlightenment regarded themselves as a courageous elite who would lead the world into progress from a long period of doubtful tradition and ecclesiastical tyranny. This dogmatism was formalized by the Protestant scholasticism of Lutheran and Calvinist divines. It was also explicit in the second scholasticism of the counter-reformation. The dogmatism was also encouraged by the idea of the "divine right of kings" which was a tenant in the Church of England.

Enlightenment thinkers reduced religion to those essentials which could only be "rationally" defended. These were certain basic moral principles and a few universally held beliefs about God. Aside from these universal principles and beliefs, religions in their particularity were largely banished from the public square. This idea was probably the idea of our "separation of church and state."

The Age of Enlightenment is considered to have ended with the French Revolution. The violent aspect of the French Revolution fostered the belief in many that Enlightenment was a curse rather than a blessing. This philosophy was usually fostered by those who wanted to return to the glory days of authority.

A new philosophy rose called Romanticism which emphasized passion, imagination and spontaneity as opposed to the dry rationality of Enlightenment. Romanticism led the way to such ideas as religious conservatism and feminism.

Enlightenment is responsible for the growth of secular humanism, economic and political liberalism, the decline of the church and the development of science. Its political thought developed the modern world. Its ideas led to democracy and capitalism. Its ideas of freedom also led to racism, nationalism, communism, and fascism.

The French Revolution

Jean Jacques Rousseau was a very influential political philosopher before the French Revolution took place. We should examine some of the tenets of his philosophy before we progress since he had some influence on the revolutionaries. He believed that human beings were born sinless but were corrupted by society. This contrasted with the ideas of the powerful Catholic Church that believed people were born in sin and could be and had to be saved.

Rousseau thought that all that is required for people to realize their full human potential was to change the social conditions under which they lived. The agent to achieve this state of perfection is government. Everyone has to subscribe to a new social contract. In order to be free, every individual has to surrender his rights to a collective body and obey the "general will." The state is vested with total power, which is legitimate because it has the consent of the majority. The general will is always right and reflects the real interests of every member of society. Anyone who disagrees with the general will is mistaken and acting contrary to his own best interests. It is the authority's responsibility to correct him and force him to act for his own benefit, to force him to be free. What is supremely important is the whole, of which an individual is merely an expendable part.

Background to the French Revolution

Before the revolution, France had no common laws or institutions of government such as were in place in England. The king was the source of all law and administrative authority, reigning by the grace of God. He was burdened by the history of his ancestors and customs which made it difficult to change things. Intellectuals tried to influence the king to change French society but could not since all the power was in the hands of the nobility who had little experience in government. To these people the ideas of the philosophers were too abstract to be understood.

Most historians agree to the following analysis. As in any political revolution the desperate action of the protesters is influenced by economic conditions as well as the welfare and safety of the individual. France, in the late eighteenth century, had been overwhelmed by the expenses of **several wars.** The burdens imposed by these wars included a huge **war debt.** This was aided by the fact that the monarchy suffered military defeats due to ineptness and ego and these resulted in a lack of social services for the huge number of war veterans as well s the general population.

There was a poor economic situation and a huge national debt caused by a **grossly inequitable** system of taxation. (If this sounds familiar, it's probably your imagination at work.)

The Roman Catholic Church was the largest landowner in the country. They levied a huge tax on the crops produced on their lands. The monarchy also increased taxes to pay for their military ineptitude. The poorest people faced a daily struggle against sickness, hunger and malnutrition.

Despite the financial burden on the populace there was continued conspicuous consumption of the noble class, especially at the court of Louis XVI and Marie-Antionette at Versailles. When told the citizens had no bread to eat, she supposedly remarked, "Then let them eat cake."

The high cost of bread coupled with unemployment caused those that did have some money to spend it on food rather than in other areas of the economy.

There was widespread famine and malnutrition in the months immediately before the Revolution. This famine was also prevalent in many other parts of Europe at the time due to poor harvests. The places that did have food were not able to get it to France due to poor transportation systems in use.

The new philosophies that were bandied about led to social and political factors involving resentment and aspiration. "Why should they have so much and I have so little?"

The average person resented the idea of royal absolutism. Merchants were honored in countries such as Germany and England but in France they were part of the servile class of citizens.

There was resentment of aristocratic housing by wage earners, peasants, and minor officials who could not afford basic housing for their families.

There was a tremendous resentment of clerical privilege as well as aspirations for freedom of religion, especially by the minority Protestant groups. Their literature was full of "Papist" resentment in the control and influence of many institutions especially education..

There was open hatred toward the King after he dismissed several financial advisers who were sympathetic to the plight of the people.

These problems were well known to the king and his advisers but they failed to do anything to correct them.

Action and Reaction

The battles of the revolution are not germane to our discussion The Revolution was originally a popular uprising against the absolute power of the king and against the privileges and wrath of the elite. It was propelled by the slogan of "liberty, equality and fraternity."

What happened after the revolution was a loss of liberty and the creation of a dictatorship. But that is another consideration, we are interested in the causes of the revolution. To put down the revolution the government is estimated to have executed up to forty thousand people.

The revolutionaries were not able to establish a durable system of governing at the turn of the century. The government changed from a republic, to a dictatorship, to a constitutional monarchy and became two different empires with a dozen different constitutions.

As a result of the French Revolution and the subsequent events a reunification of Germany took place for its own protection from France. The revolution inspired Bolsheviks in Russia to emulate their techniques and used the French precedent of large scale executions of the "enemies of the people."

Not everyone in France supported the revolution. As the saying goes, "there were too many monarchists to have a republic and too many republicans to have a monarchy."

The revolution did emphasize the concepts of being a citizen with rights and that the state belonged to its citizens. The revolution created the concept of nationalism.

It affirmed that it was morally right to overthrow the existing order by force on the grounds of **abstract principles rather than existing laws.** All that was needed was to seize the power and use it for the benefit of society.

The role of the Catholic Church in causing the revolution is worth considering. The church was immensely powerful. It had a monopoly on public worship and Protestants had no civil rights. It controlled the educational system, poor relief funds, hospital provision and had extensive powers of censorship. Most young people of the United States are not old enough to remember or even heard of "Banned in Boston."

The pulpit was used by the secular authorities for announcements and to keep the king's subjects docile and obedient. There developed a strong anti-clerical reaction to the intolerance of the church.

The revolutionaries tried to make a complete break with the past and create an entirely rational society purged entirely of Christianity and based on the idea of deism. People were given a new identity as citizens of the state. Loyalty to the State was the citizen's highest duty. In this way the revolution changed peoples beliefs, identity and values. Citizenship was a universal office, everyone was to serve the community and the country.

The Failed Russian Revolution of 1905

In December 1904, a strike occurred at major railway and an artillery supplier in Saint Petersburg. Sympathy strikes in other parts of the city raised the number of strikers to over 80,000. A controversial Orthodox priest, who headed a police-sponsored workers' association, led a huge workers' procession to the Winter Palace to deliver a petition to the Tsar on Sunday, 9 January 1905. The troops guarding the Winter Palace who had been ordered to tell the demonstrators not to pass a certain point, opened fire on them, which resulted in nearly 1000 deaths. The event became known as Bloody Sunday and is usually considered the start of the active phase of the

1905 Revolution. However, there had been hundreds of peaceful protests of citizens before this event.

The events in Saint Petersburg provoked public indignation and a series of massive strikes that spread quickly throughout the industrial centers of the Russian Empire. Poland was under Russian rule and Polish socialists called for a general strike. By the end of January 1905, over 400,000 workers in the country were on strike. Half of European Russia's industrial workers went on strike in 1905, as well as almost all workers in Poland. There were also strikes in Ukraine as well as in the Baltic coast countries, also under Russian domination. In Riga, 80 protesters were killed on 26 January 1905, and in Warsaw a few days later over 100 strikers were shot on the streets. By February, there were strikes in the Caucasus and by April in the Urals and beyond. In March, all higher academic institutions were forcibly closed for the remainder of the year, adding radical students to the striking workers.

A strike by railway workers on 21 October 1905 quickly developed into a general strike in Saint Petersburg and Moscow. This prompted the setting up of the short-lived Soviet of Workers' Deputies a largely Menshevik group led by Leon Trotsky which organized strike action in over 200 factories. By 26 October 1905, over 2 million workers were on strike and there were almost no active railways in all of Russia. Growing inter-ethnic confrontation throughout the Caucasus resulted in Armenian massacres, heavily damaging the cities and the Baku oilfields.

With the unsuccessful and bloody War with Japan,(1904–1905), there was unrest in army reserve units. On January 2, 1905 Port Arthur in the far east was lost, and the Russian fleet was crippled in several engagements. In February 1905, the Russian army was defeated at Tsushima, losing almost 80,000 men in the process.

In 1905, there were naval mutinies peaking in June with the mutiny aboard the Battleship Ptomkin. Some sources claim over 2,000 sailors died in the restoration of order. The mutinies were disorganized and quickly crushed. Despite these mutinies, the armed forces were largely apolitical and remained mostly loyal to the Tsar and were widely used by the government to control the 1905 unrest.

Nationalist groups had been angered by the crackdown on dissidents. The Poles, Finns, and the Baltic provinces all sought autonomy, and also freedom to use their national languages and promote their own culture. Muslim groups were also active and the First Congress of the Muslim Union took place in August 1905. Certain groups took the opportunity to settle differences with each other rather than the government. Some nationalists undertook anti-Jewish action, possibly with government aid, and over 3000 Jews were killed.

The number of prisoners throughout the Russian Empire, which had peaked at 116,376 in 1893, fell by over a third to a record low of 75,009 in January 1905, chiefly because of several mass amnesties granted by the Tsar. One must wonder what role these released criminals played in the 1905–6 social unrest.

The Tsar dismissed the Minister of the Interior and appointed a government commission "to inquire without delay into the causes of discontent among the workers in the city of St Petersburg and its suburbs" in view of the strike movement. It was also meant to have included workers' delegates elected according to a two-stage system. Elections of the workers delegates were, however, blocked by the socialists who wanted to divert the workers from the elections to the armed struggle. The Commission was dissolved without having started work.

Following the assassination of his uncle, the Tsar agreed to give new concessions. He published a document which promised the formation of a consultative assembly, religious tolerance, freedom of speech (in the form of language rights for the Polish minority) and a reduction in the peasants' redemption payments. The Tsar confirmed his promise to convene an assembly of people's representatives.

The Tsar agreed to the creation of citizens legislature but with consultative powers only. When its slight powers and limits on the electorate were revealed, unrest redoubled. The Soviet, a workers organization, was formed and called for a general strike in October and encouraged refusal to pay taxes and the withdrawal of bank deposits.

A petition manifesto was presented to the Tsar on 14 October. It closely followed the demands of the petitions of September, granting basic human rights, allowing the formation of political parties, extending the franchise towards free bargaining, and establishing the Duma as the central legislative body. The Tsar waited and argued for three days, but finally signed the manifesto on 30 October 1905, owing to his desire to avoid a massacre, and a realization that there was insufficient military force available to do otherwise. He regretted signing the document, saying that he felt "sick with shame at this betrayal of the dynasty he had inherited," and that " the betrayal was complete".

When the manifesto was proclaimed there were spontaneous demonstrations of support in all the major cities. The strikes in St. Petersburg and elsewhere officially ended or quickly collapsed. A political amnesty was also offered. The concessions came hand-in-hand with renewed, and brutal action against the continued unrest. There was also a backlash from the conservative elements of society, with right-wing attacks on strikers, left-wingers, and Jews.

While the Russian liberals were satisfied by the Tsar's actions they took preparations for upcoming Dumas elections as radical socialists and revolutionaries denounced the elections and called for an armed uprising to destroy the Empire.

Some of the November uprising of 1905 was directed against the government, while some was undirected. It included terrorism, worker strikes, peasant unrest, and military mutinies and was only suppressed after fierce battles. The railroad fell into the hands of striker committees and demobilized soldiers returning from the east. The Tsar had to send a special detachment of loyal troops along the Trans Siberian Railway to restore order. A train was overturned by striking workers at the main railway depot in St. Petersburg.

Unrest continued well into December There was a general strike by Russian workers in the capital. The government sent in troops and a bitter street fight ensued. Finally after a week of battle a special regiment was sent in which used artillery to break-up demonstrations and to shell workers' living areas. After about a thousand deaths and parts of the city in ruins the workers surrendered. Similar uprisings in Moscow were also destroyed.

The Tsar finally had the bulk of his military under control and it was obvious to the dissidents that they should retreat and fight another day.

According to figures presented in the Duma by a Professor Kovalesky, more than 14,000 people had been executed and 75,000 imprisoned in the failed rebellion.

The Successful Russian Revolution of 1917

Many people confuse the Russian Revolution of 1917 with the takeover of Russia by the Bolsheviks and the Russian Civil War. The Tsar had abdicated before the civil war broke out. The war was a struggle for the power vacuum left by the abdication of the Tsar. The revolution had already been concluded and a Provisional Government was in place consisting of a coalition of competing groups. About a dozen of these groups were of sufficient size to wield some power.

The Bolsheviks were a minority group for most of the years leading up to the abdication of the Tsar. Their successful tactic was to infiltrate community leadership groups and take them over. The workers organizations were known as Soviets. The Soviets were usually represented by members from the different factions such as Mensheviks, Cadets, Cossacks, Socialist Revolutionaries and of course Bolsheviks. An example of the success of Bolshevik tactics is illustrated in the city of Tula in 1917. Bolsheviks represented about 25 percent of the population, but their representation in the Soviet was 76 percent, so they had the power to pass any proposal and the power to defeat any proposal..

In many societies there is a ruling power structure that is not necessarily large but strong enough to keep control, usually with the support of the police and military. When the power becomes sufficiently excessive in its repression of the people under its rule then it is ripe for revolution. When many of the repressed people are willing to sacrifice their lives to end the repression a successful overturn of leadership will usually be the result.

Tsar Alexander II of Russia decreed in 1861 that the serfs were no longer part of the property of the land owners. Most of the serfs stayed on and worked the land as renters or share croppers. Most of the lands were worked for many decades by the ancestors of the now free serfs so they held a special attachment to the land, their blood was in the soil. After the freedom of the serfs was granted the gentry of the land still provided the Tsar with taxes and soldiers for his military adventures from those on the estate. Not only did the aristocratic families own the land but they also had relatives in high government offices.

Shortly after their emancipation many of the younger members of the serf families slowly began migrating to the city where more opportunities prevailed than in the country. Factory jobs provided comparatively high income as well as a more exciting life than back on the farm.

As a result of this slow migration to the cities the production of food was diminished and a crises developed. Non-Russian groups, such as Poles and Ukrainians, resented the movement of their food to Moscow and St. Petersburg. The largest of these non-Russian groups were the Poles, Ukrainians, and the Baltic peoples of Estonia, Latvia and Lithuania.

When the war with Japan broke out in 1904 it was assumed the Russians would smash the Japanese, especially since the Trans-Siberian Railway had been completed ten years previously. The Russians were defeated, forced to sign a treaty and gave up territory. This signaled a weak military state to the rest of the world as well as to the citizens of Russia.

The militant city groups such as industrial workers, transportation workers and military detachments began to resist taxes and government control. Many members of the military deserted. On the farm, many estates were looted and then burned. The owners fled to safety. This was in 1905-06.

Large groups of people would gather in the streets of St. Petersburg demanding bread, shorter working hours and for the Tsar to abdicate. One such group numbering about 20,000 were simply shot up by the Tsar's loyal troops. An estimated 1500 people were killed. In the Tsar's diary that night he wrote, "there was some trouble up at Nevsky Prospect."

Finally the Tsar prevailed and many executions took place as expedient trials were conducted in the revolutionary areas.

Thousands of peasants who had confiscated aristocratic housing and lands were executed.

After the bloodbath of 1906 there were many groups, both open and secret, who plotted the overthrow of the Tsar. These groups coordinated their efforts and kept in touch with each other. Most of their leaders had been imprisoned at one time or another. Vladimir Ulyanov, who became Lenin, was in exile in Siberia then he fled the country and was out of Russia for seventeen years before he returned to lead the Bolsheviks.

When Russia entered World War I, it did so with one of the poorest equipped armies in the history of warfare. The Tsar and his advisers entered the war with the idea that an Allied victory over the central powers would give them complete control of the Black Sea and the important Dardanelles water passage to the Mediterranean Sea, which was held by the Turks at the time.

There was a general conscription of men for the military from the peasantry as well as from the city. Not many of the conscripts supported the war as thousands of letter documents of the times attested. In the first year of the war many of the soldiers trained with wooden guns or sticks. Many of them were sent into battle without ever having fired a gun. Many were sent into battle with the idea they would pick up a gun from a fallen soldier.

Russian army leadership was not prepared for modern warfare of the time with machine guns and sophisticated heavy artillery as well as mobile transport. They were still under the allure of horses and sabers. Airplanes were an entirely new weapon.

Thousands of Russian soldiers were killed in the first battles of the war. Thousands deserted the front and became a criminal element as they made their way back to their cities and farms.

Meanwhile Tsar Nicholas II seemed at a loss at what to do. He shuffled the military leadership deck. He even went to the front to take command of the army even though he had no military experience.

The Empress Alexandra took command of the government in St. Petersburg (now Petrograd) with the mysterious holy man Rasputin as her adviser. Her superstitious attachment to Rasputin was the subject of much gossip by the public.

There were many attempts before the war to get Tsar Nicholas to agree to a Duma which would act as an advisory body or quasi-legislature. He agreed and it was formed only to be scraped at the Tsar's whim. It was formed, dissolved, and reformed. The Tsar did not want a democratic monarchy such as England had at the time. Even before the Tsar went to the front there were demonstrations in Petrograd where protesting crowds of a hundred thousand or more were common. These demonstrations were usually scattered by the arrival of troops who didn't mind shooing into the crowd.

These protesters and marchers had high hopes for their local worker organizations called Soviets. There were also Coalition Councils in the cities which were designed to bring order to protests and cooperation among the many groups other than the Soviets. As the Tsar's grip on the population waned the Coalition Council became the ruling body (Provisional Government) and the rabble crowd more or less waited for their instructions.

The Provisional Government formally took over the Russian government in February 1917. The Tsar abdicated on 3 March 1917. The Interim coalition government promised to hold general elections in November. The Bolsheviks now had the support of many of the Soviet councils. They were the only major political party who advocated pulling out of the war which enhanced their popularity.

Fearing that the November elections might bring cohesion to the county the Bolsheviks made a desperate move in October and arrested the members of the Provisional Government in the name of the people and the Soviet (worker's councils.) This was the official take over of the revolutionaries.

It was not long before troops, called Red Guards, commanded by the Bolsheviks, were firing on crowds in Petrograd. The Bolshevik leaders were all familiar with the events of the French Revolution and often cited their techniques in their speeches and correspondence..

After the official end of the revolution a civil war broke out with the Bolsheviks on one side (Reds) and a coalition of their opponents on the other (Whites). The Reds prevailed and immediately engaged in a Red Terror to subdue and frighten the population.

The Cuban Revolution – 1956

The Cuban Revolution of 1956 was a peasant uprising against the regime of Fulgencio Batista y Zaldiyar who was closely aligned with and supported by the United States. He rose to power in 1933 when he was part of a group that overthrew the authoritarian rule of Gerardo Machado. Batista appointed himself chief of the armed forces with the rank of colonel and effectively controlled a five member coalition presidency. He maintained this control until 1940 when he was elected President of Cuba. Among his supporters were the Cuban communists and the labor unions. He instituted a Constitution of Cuba which was considered advanced for its time and conditions of the country. He finished his term in 1944 then went to live in the United States. He returned to Cuba in 1952 to run for the presidency again. He was certain to lose the election and collecting old personal debts led a military coup that preempted the election.

Since his takeover was obvious to everyone in the country, in order to secure his power, he had to revoke several forward looking laws that he helped previously to set in place. He prohibited the right to strike and curtailed all political activity. In essence he abandoned the Constitution. After shackling the citizenry he went into partnership with the wealthy landowners who were mostly foreigners and who used the land for sugar production rather than for producing food for the citizenry. The gap between rich and poor was staggering.

To further their wealth, members of the regime began negotiating with American crime bosses who controlled gambling, drugs, and prostitution in Havana and other large cities. He further made agreements with his American investors who operated resort areas, hotels and the tourist industry.

When small groups of student protesters became larger Batista moved to tighter censorship of the media and expelled some foreign correspondents who appeared unfriendly to his regime. He began to utilize American supplied arms and secret police who used torture and public executions as a means of quelling critics. In this rampage the best estimates are that more than twenty thousand people were executed. Murdered?

When his regime was finally defeated by the revolutionaries, among them Fidel Castro, Batista fled to the Dominican Republic where he came under the military protection of Rafael Trujillo, himself a stern dictator. Eventually Batista received political asylum in Portugal. He died of a heart attack in 1973 at the age of 72.

The United States seems to always be on the wrong side of a revolution that occurs in other parts of the world. The obsession with communism spurred on by the McCarthy witch hunts clouded our rationality. Did anyone really believe a communist dictatorship could take over the United States in some manner?

Rather than work with the Castro revolutionaries we immediately made them our enemy. We also made him a communist dictator. We allowed thousands of Batista's henchmen into our country. The college where I was teaching immediately hired two of them and put them in the Language Department. President Kennedy inherited the mess from President Eisenhower. Once again, American business interests seemed to be the driving force behind our support of a corrupt regime. Even today we let the Cuban exiles dictate our policies toward Cuba to the detriment of both countries.

In an interview on 24 October 1963 President John F. Kennedy stated "I believe that there is no country in the world including any and all the countries under colonial domination, where economic colonization, humiliation and exploitation were worse than in Cuba, in part owing to my country's policies during the Batista regime. I approved the proclamation which Fidel Castro made in the Sierra Maestra, when he justifiably called for justice and especially yearned to rid Cuba of corruption. I will even go further: to some extent it is as though Batista was the incarnation of a number of sins on the part of the United States. Now we shall have to pay for those sins. In the matter of the Batista regime, I am in agreement with the first Cuban revolutionaries. That is perfectly clear."

Events of the Cuban Revolution

On July 26, 1953, a group of approximately one hundred poorly armed revolutionaries attacked the Moncada Barracks. Many of them were killed in the battles after the attack. The survivors, among them Fidel Castro Ruz and his brother Raoúl Castro, were captured shortly after the battle. In a highly political trial, they were sentenced to long prison terms. Fidel Castro was sentenced to 15 years in an island prison. \

In 1955, due to pressure from civil leaders, the general opposition, and the priest who had helped educate Fidel Castro, and perhaps because he had known the Castro brothers in their youth, Batista freed all political prisoners, including the Moncada attackers. The Castro brothers went into exile in Mexico, where they gathered more exiled Cubans to fight in the Cuban revolution for the overthrow of Batista. During that period, Castro also met the Argentine doctor Che Guevera, who joined their forces. They were trained by Alberto Bayo, a former military leader of the failed "loyalists" in the Spanish Civil War.

The group of 80 revolutionaries training in Mexico under the leadership of Fidel Castro left for Cuba in November 1956, in a small yacht. They hoped their landing in Eastern Cuba would coincide with planned uprisings in the cities and a general strike which was planned by underground groups. It was their intention to launch an armed offensive and swiftly topple the Batista government.

The ship was delayed in getting to Cuba. It arrived too late for a coordinated attack with the island revolutionaries. After landing and realizing they had missed their opportunity they headed into the mountains of Southeastern Cuba. Batista had heard of the exiled groups return and sent an army battalion into the mountains to get them. Most of the arriving revolutionaries were killed and the

survivors were estimated at less than twenty five who had scattered in all directions.

Eventually the survivors were reunited with the help of peasant sympathizers. This small group which included Fidel Castro, Raoul Castro, Ernesto Che Guevara and Camilo Cienfuegos would form the core of the guerrilla army leadership.

Castro forces were quite small in the beginning, usually less than 200 at any one time while Batista had an army of between 30 and 40,000 soldiers. This was enforced by a large number of police. However, the government forces were reluctant to leave the city life and go into the mountains. Batista used bloody repression to keep control of the cities. He was successful in that enterprise up until the end when he fled the country.

Meanwhile up in the mountains the forces led by Castro had their own set of terror techniques. They executed many supporters of the regime and eventually won control of the mountains. Among those executed were also other revolutionaries who were a threat to the leadership of Castro.

Castro also had help from many revolutionary groups thrown together by disgruntled groups of sugar cane workers, students, and unemployed urbanites. These hastily thrown groups did not control any land but had caused enough problems for the regime that they aided Castro enough to make a difference. These groups were able to supply Castro with military movements and other intelligence. They also protected the supply lines of food and arms that were going to Castro by diverting government forces to engage them in conflicts.\

The war had been in progress for two years when the United States government on March 14, 1958 imposed an arms embargo on the Cuban government. This included airplanes as well as airplane parts. The airplane was one of Batista's best weapons.

Batista decided to attack the mountains full force. He sent a detachment of twelve thousand solders into the hills, most of them were untrained recruits. Castro engineered small scale battles rather than direct confrontations. In one skirmish called the Battle of La Plata which lasted ten days, Castro's forces killed over a thousand of their enemy, captured 240 prisoners with the loss of only three of their own fighters. However, in a later battle known as the Battle of Las Mercedes Castro lost 70 troops out of a total of 300 who had entered the battle. What had happened was General Cantillo of the government forces had lured Castro into a trap. Castro asked Cantillo for a cease fire and was given this condition in order to engage in negotiations. With cunning Castro and his survivors escaped back into the mountains.

Che Guervera issued the following statement: "The enemy soldier in the Cuban example which at present concerns us, is the junior partner of the dictator; he is the man who gets the last crumb left by a long line of profiteers that begins in Havana and ends with him. He is disposed to defend his privileges, but he is disposed to defend them only to the degree that they are important to him. His salary and his pension are worth some suffering and some dangers, but they are never worth his life. If the price of maintaining them will cost it, he is better off giving them up; that is to say, withdrawing from the battle." Che Guevara, guerrilla commander, 1958

It was the end of summer in 1958 when Castro's forces grew large enough to launch an offensive. Castro opened an offensive on four fronts hoping to split the government response into smaller units in each area of combat. Other resistant groups, not under the command of Castro, joined the offensive. A number of cities came under control of the revolutionaries in this offensive. The revolutionaries were usually greeted warmly by the inhabitants.

By the end of the year Batista could not take the intensity of the defeats and no longer had authority over much of his army that were interested in their own survival. He left Cuba for the Dominican Republic on January 1, 1959.

Once Batista had fled, Castro appealed to the commander of the army in Santiago de Cuba to negotiate. The commander simply ordered his troops to lay down their arms and Castro took over this very important city. The forces commanded by Guevara and Cienfuegos entered Havana on the same day, January 2, 1959. Castro arrived in Havana on January 6 and was at the head of a victory march. A new interim president was installed, but Castro was firmly in control.

After the Victory

When Castro's group took over the government they arrested suspected Batista sympathizers, policemen, soldiers and former public officials and charged them with human rights abuses and war crimes as well as torture and murder. Most of those convicted were given long prison sentences and those convicted of murder were executed by firing squads. They were particularly sensitive to those who might be able to form a counter-revolution. They also exiled many former army officers rather than execute them.

In 1961, after the Bay of Pigs Invasion, the new Cuban government also confiscated all property held by religious organizations without compensation. Hundreds of members of the clergy, including a bishop, were permanently expelled from the nation, with the new Cuban government being officially atheist. Many competing former rebel leaders were forced into exile. \

Castro nationalized all foreign owned businesses and those held by upper class Cubans. This included the plantation owned by the Castro family. The United States placed an embargo on Cuba which is still in force at this writing.

After the Cuban missile crisis was successfully handled by President Kennedy the United States promised that it would not invade the land of Cuba. The United States maintained the island area known as Guantanamo which is presently a thorn in the side of the Cuban government.

III A PROTEST STUDY

All human beings are born free and equal in dignity and rights. They are endowed with reason and conscience and should act towards one another in a spirit of brotherhood.

Group Safety

The most important issue to an individual is survival with an optimum comfort of living. Comfort, somehow, goes against the nature of living since it is discomfort that creates progress. We seem to have a lot of discomfort lately so we should be making progress. We are making slow progress with the emphasis on slow.

There had been great strides made in the late 1930s in reducing the pain of people during the Great Depression. World War II increased the number of people in what became known as the middle class. Most of this was due to the rise in Union membership as well as the creation of new unions. The American aristocracy began to bad-mouth unions and compared them to the criminal element in society.

Don't think for one minute that the owners of railroads, coal mines and steel mills went along willingly with the demands made by unions. They hired thugs as strike breakers, put pressure on legislators and corrupted law enforcement in order to keep labor in servitude.

After a post-war campaign to destroy the power of unions, that is, the power of the people, they succeeded in destroying most of the strength of the unions. It took about thirty years and in the early 1980s the decline, not only of union,s but of the wages and life styles of the working class began.

If we are to take back the country, all working people, all minimum wage workers, have got to join a union, council, or association of some kind related to their work. There should be a coordination of these associations with support for each other. The members of the association must follow their leadership if they wish to make progress. Debate the issue before making a move.

There are other organizations, not connected with labor, that attempt to influence legislation for the betterment of all citizens. These keep an eye on Social Security, Medicare and health care as well as environmental issues. You have to come up with a few bucks and support at least one of these in their efforts. Be wary, some of these organizations look good on paper, but some of them are designed to provide employment for the organizers and only a small fraction of the proceeds go to their purpose or cause. Most of these are exposed on the internet.

Be assured, for every organization with a good social cause, there is a counter-organization to combat that cause. It is a good example of survival of the fittest at the best level. Generally, the counter-organization is one backed by big money and their cause is making more money or protecting what they already have. It is difficult to find out who are the financiers of the many patriotic sounding organizations that publish slanted opinions.

If it is difficult for you to join a union, then seek out some other organization concerning your employment. Start a WalMart group even if it is not a union. Have regular meetings and a summer picnic or a group day at the park or amusement center. The main thing is to get organized and stay organized. Discuss political candidates or at least legislative issues that might affect your employment. Let our slogan be "Power to the People." Put it on your organization letterhead. Put it on the back of your correspondence.

It is easier to influence a legislator than an entrepreneur if you are talking progress in the work place. This is not referring to a small restaurant owner or a miniature golf enterprise. This comment is for the leaders of industry, corporate executives and other business managers. These people have a squadron of lawyers, influence with police and are backed by high finance to intimidate and subdue. We can only counter this bastion of power by sheer numbers.

Don't protest voting by not voting. When the Tsar abdicated there were about twenty political groups with large membership. They formed a general assembly and an interim government with rules and regulations set down. This was to rule the country until general elections could be held. The Bolsheviks were in the minority. They used tactics in the general assembly that dragged the meetings on and on. They were so obnoxious to the other members that two large groups, Mensheviks and Social Revolutionaries, walked out of the legislative session. Bad Idea! This gave the Bolsheviks enough of a majority to quickly ram through legislation that gave them a huge political advantage.

Bucharin, one of the Bolshevik leaders referred to, "the constitutional allusions which are still alive in the masses" Another observer of the process wrote, "carried on by ideals...they believed the 'will of the people" was enough to defend its democratic institutions. Democratic leaders placed so much faith in democratic methods they failed to see how the Bolsheviks undemocratic methods could succeed in the long run."

Register to vote and vote, using your organization recommendations as a guideline. Register as an Independent in order to send a message to our two dominant political parties. Deviation from a membership block vote might satisfy an ego, but it is not a good idea.

Memberships - NRA example

Since I have passed my eightieth year I have had the opportunity to belong to many organizations other than unions. Since the environment was my passion and my area of alleged expertise about half of these organizations were connected with that interest. Many organizations were more like contributions to a cause such as March of Dimes, Salvation Army, NAACP and medical research groups.

When my membership ran out on one of these latter groups I would shift to some other with the same type of objectives. For a few years I was with the Wilderness Society, then a few with the Sierra Club, then World Wildlife Fund and many years with the National Wildlife Federation. This way, I spread my limited resources around.

A very interesting membership was with the National Rifle Association. I looked upon my membership as a "hobby" just like my membership in my local Stamp Club. I used some of their literature when I edited a book, "Beginners Shooting Guide" which was a compilation of the writings of several different authors.

I was willing to debate the Second Amendment with others. One guy had me on the ropes with his argument that the Second Amendment didn't protect our right to own guns for hunting. As usual, I left that membership and switched to Ducks Unlimited.

The NRA holds its membership together with the idea that the government, or somebody, wants to take away our guns.They usually support Republicans even though Democrats like Harry Reid are strong supporters of "gun rights." Why is that?

Once when my wife asked me why I had so many guns I said that a gun was a beautiful example of the ingenuity of human invention and the human mind. Agony! She didn't quite like that response. Then later I said, "You never know when we will have to defend ourselves against our own government." She went into double agony over that remark.

This brings me to my point. There are four members of the NRA in my circle of acquaintances. Every one of them believes our government is their enemy - every one of them. I wonder if this is true of the entire NRA membership. If it is, then I wonder what it means.

Wisconsin Protests of 2011

The protests in Wisconsin are an excellent example of a problem and how people used protesting as a method of solving that problem. Some of their methods did not work and some did.

In the first half of 2011 there were a series of protests and demonstrations in the state of Wisconsin concerning a bill proposed by the governor, Scott Walker, called the Budget Repair Bill. Tens of thousands of protestors were on the streets of the capital city letting their feelings be known as objecting to curtailment of union activity as specified in the document. These protesters were soon joined by counter-protesters made up of anti-tax activists and conservatives. The first protesters wanted to keep the status quo while the counter-protesters wanted government spending reduced.

The bill would seriously curtail state-paid workers (including teachers) medical benefits and make it illegal for them to negotiate with the state as a consolidated group. Removing the labor union's right to collective bargaining will effectively render them useless organizations. The governor claimed he was most concerned with balancing his budget, he wouldn't budge on outlawing collective bargaining.

The collective bargaining bill was signed into law. It was struck down by a Wisconsin court saying it violated the Open Meetings Law. The state supreme court overturned the lower courts ruling.

The number of protesters in February was estimated at over twenty five thousand. By June the number protesting was less than a thousand but the dialogue and accusations continued at a brisk pace. Various law suits against the law were initiated.

The main controversy of the bill was its proposal of taking away the ability of public sector unions to bargain collectively over health care, pensions and limiting raises of public employees to the rate of inflation. It also involved the state's collection of union dues. The bargaining agreement exempted the unions of public safety officers, including police, state troopers and fire fighters. Without the legislation the governor said that thousands of state workers would be laid off.

After reading about the benefits of the Wisconsin state and education workers one would have to agree that the retirement and health benefits were generous and paid for by the taxpayers and not really by the employees. For instance, many school districts paid for the entire dental and health policies of their employees. No contribution from the workers was taken. As to pensions here's a quote, "The Wisconsin state pension plan requires a 6.8% employer contribution and 6.2% from the employee. However, according to collective bargaining agreements in place since 1996, the districts pay the employees share as well, for a total of 13%. One district also contributed an additional 4.2% of teacher salaries to cover a second pension and teachers contribute nothing." *Wikipedia*

Another proposal in the Budget Repair bill was to diminish legislature oversight on implementation and eligibility requirements for the state's Medicare programs. There was also a clause that would allow the state to sell up to 37 of its heating and cooling plants without competitive bids. A group of internet investigators called Anonymous claimed this was a move to sell state owned property to political contributors at bargain basement prices.

The bill was passed 57 to 17 with 28 representatives not voting, although many of them claimed to have failed in trying to vote since the time of the vote lasted less than fifteen seconds. Several said their voting buttons did not function properly.

Some highlights of the Wisconsin protest. During the week of February 14 more than 30,000 protesters were active in the streets. Protests spread to Ohio where a similar bill was being considered. Richard Trumka and other AFL-CIO leaders addressed the protest crowd on February 18. Trumka said the plan was part of a larger national Republican strategy. Protesting numbers were now estimated at 70,000.

A website "Defend Wisconsin" was set up to coordinate rallies, publish video footage and provide general information about the subject.

On February 26, the protesting numbers grew to an estimated 100,000. At this time supporting protests were held in other state capitals. One of the Wisconsin public union groups filed an unfair labor practices complaint asserting that the governor had a duty to negotiate but refused.

By March, things were getting near a boiling point. The governor threatened to send lay off notices to 1,500 state employees if the bill was not passed. Michael Moore addressed a crowd of "tens of thousands" He said, "The country is awash in wealth and cash. It's just that its not in your hands. It has been transferred, in the greatest heist in history, from the working and consumer class to the banks and portfolios of the (super) rich."

A hacker group calling itself Anonymous publicized a little-noticed clause in the bill proposed by Walker which would allow the state to sell its utilities to anyone it chose, at any price, without the public even being notified. This clause would allow companies like Koch Industries to purchase publicly owned utility plants, and Anonymous believed this is the reason that Koch-funded "grassroots" organizations like Americans For Prosperity, Club for Growth and

Citizens United who are supporting Walker's plan to rid the unions of their collective power.

The groups just mentioned are designed to give the impression that they are concerned about the welfare of the country and its citizens. They are merely tools of the wealthy aimed at keeping them in power and limiting benefits to the average citizen under the guise of fiscal responsibility.

The news and comments continued: On March 9, Wisconsin Republicans passed legislation to limit state workers' collective bargaining rights, and a special conference committee of state lawmakers approved the bill a short time later. The Senate requires a quorum to take up any measures that spend money, however by removing parts of the bill related to money, they had discovered a way to bypass the chamber's missing Democrats.

Post-passage reactions

On March 11, Governor Walker signed the bill and put out a statement rescinding layoff notices for 1,500 public workers. He said the bill's passage "helped us save 1,500 middle-class jobs by moving forward this week with the budget repair. The state will now be able to realize $30 million in savings to balance the budget and allow 1,500 state employees to keep their jobs."

In response a lawsuit was filed against the state regarding the bill, stating that it was unconstitutionally passed because the budget repair bill contained fiscal provisions.

On March 12, the fourteen Democratic senators who had left the state returned and were met by crowds of between 85,000 to 185,000, the largest crowds yet of the four weeks of protests. Teachers, police, firefighters, nurses, and students were joined by farmers who paraded their farm vehicles around Capitol Square. One of the returning senators said that "we are back to unite and fight with our supporters. We gave them hope. They gave us inspiration." In contrast, the senate majority leader said that the returning senators were "the most shameful 14 people in the state of Wisconsin. They were an absolute insult to the hundreds of thousands of

Wisconsinites who are struggling to find a job, much less one they can run away from and go down to Illinois."

On March 25, a lawsuit was filed against the state alleging that the budget repair bill still contained budget provisions, and hence was unlawfully passed by the state as it would have required a quorum. Also on March 25, after meeting with Senate Republicans, the Legislative Reference Bureau bypassed the Secretary of State's office and officially published the collective bargaining law. There had been a court-issued restraining order restricting its publication, but the order was issued against the Secretary of State's office instead of the Bureau. According to the director of the Bureau, the publication is a purely ministerial act that forwards the bill to the Secretary of State; the bill needs to be published by the Secretary of State to become law. Despite this, Republicans say that the bill is officially law and they plan to enforce it. A legal ruling was made that an "arm of the state could not sue the state."

On April 9, demonstrators marched from the Capitol to the offices of the state business lobby, Wisconsin Manufacturers and Commerce. The action was sparked in part by attention given to Charles and David Koch, billionaire brothers who support Wisconsin's Republican Gov. Walker and have spent millions of dollars on conservative causes.

On April 13, the Board of Education announced punishments ranging from one-day unpaid suspensions up to 15 days for teachers who called in sick on February 18, forcing their schools to close, at the height of the protests over the budget repair bill.

On April 20, the Department of Natural Resources reported costs for personnel involved in the demonstrations topped $350,000, and the parking tab for police to park their vehicles approached $100,000.

On April 28, it was reported that some of the doctors at the University of Wisconsin who gave out sick notes to union supporters skipping work to protest would face punishment ranging from written reprimands to docked pay and loss of leadership positions. The Medical Examining Board and state Department of Licensing and Regulation are also investigating the doctors.

On May 11, a dozen protesters chanted, "Stand up, fight back" in the Senate gallery, **forcing the Senate to recess** while protesters were removed. Much the same occurred in the Assembly as the body passed the voter ID bill. A repeat of events occurred throughout the week, ending with protesters crashing a news conference held by Senate Republicans following the passage of the voter ID bill. The tactics have irritated both Democrats and Republicans. Capitol police arrested several protesters, but it did not deter a core group that kept returning.

On May 12, 100 pages of public records were released that detailed the emotions and threats that occurred during the protests. Dozens of emails suggested Walker or legislators should be shot, or hanged, or should watch their backs, look over their shoulders or resign. The records show that FBI agents from Maine to California to Florida also got involved.

On May 14, the Wisconsin Department of Administration estimated cleanup and overtime costs for the protests will reach about $8 million which includes $270,000 for interior and exterior Capitol building repairs._The same day, between 10,000 to 15,000 protesters participated in a rally protesting the collective bargaining bill, education cuts, cuts and immigrant rights. Christian Pacheco, a graduating high school senior, revealed at the protest that he was a student. "My dream is to work hard and go to a UW school just like my peers," said Pacheco. "If I am forced to pay out of state tuition, out of my pocket, as Walker's budget proposes this dream will be crushed." The crowd chanted in support of Pacheco who had the status of illegal immigrant.

Protesters began living in tents around the capitol in a complex they deemed "Walkerville" around the time the 2012 fiscal year budget was being debated. The budget, which would turn a $3.6 billion deficit into a $300 million surplus in 5 years, drew harsh criticism from union members and protesters as it cut approximately $800 million in education, and allowed the private school choice program to be expanded.

Around 3 a.m. on June 16, the Wisconsin State Assembly passed the 2012 fiscal year budget with a party line vote of 60-38. During the Senate debate, an onlooker was removed after screaming repeatedly at a Republican Senator while he was speaking. The Senate subsequently approved the 2012 fiscal year budget later that day, with a party line vote of 19-14. Shortly after the vote, an onlooker repeatedly screamed "I want my Democracy back!" and others screamed repeatedly "Kill the bill!". The screaming onlookers were removed shortly, except for the ones who chained themselves to the railing who were later arrested.

On June 21, a pro-union protester was punched in the face at a daily Capitol singalong. Two men who were not a part of the Capitol singalong came in and began to drag a Tea Party *Don't Tread on Me* flag over some of the singers' heads. One of the singers tried to grab the flag to stop them, and he was punched in the face and suffered a broken tooth. The two counter-protesters were also joined by a former Republican State Senator , who was seen yelling at the singers and attempting to run over their belongings with his wheelchair.

Decline in protests

Matthew Rothschild, editor of a magazine said "People see that Walker won everything big that he asked for, and despite all the great activism, we don't have anything to show for it. The mass protests that I expected this week at the capitol in Madison did not materialize." By June 14, the number of protesters at the Capital was approximately 5,000 and by June 16 the number was down to about 1,000.

Law enforcement actions

When first announcing the budget repair bill on February 11, Walker said that state agencies were prepared for any fallout including a walk-out by state prison guards. Although unable to cross state lines, officers were sent to find the fleeing lawmakers. The City of Madison Police Spokesman Joel DeSpain issued a press-release on March 5, noting for the third weekend in a row that demonstrations had been peaceful. He said that there has been no arrests and no citations during the start of the weekend (March 4 and 5) where tens of thousands of protesters were present.

In April, Katherine R. Windels, aged 26, was charged with two felonies for allegedly sending death-threat emails to Republican state Senators.

On June 8, a dozen silent demonstrators wearing zombie makeup and protest T-shirts were arrested after lying down on the floor of a legislator's Capitol offices and refusing to leave. Police carried out the demonstrators "one by one."

On June 16, two protesters were arrested after locking themselves onto the Senate gallery railing with bike locks. Later in the day six other people in the Capitol had been arrested on allegations of disorderly conduct.

Some unions were hoping to beat the deadline for the state's new collective bargaining law and get a new deal done. For example, the Brown Deer School Board called for an emergency meeting the night before the budget repair law became effective to see if it could reach a last minute deal with the teachers union. Dozens of Brown Deer taxpayers worried the board was going to rush through a teachers' contract before the law became effective. When asked if the teachers union was trying to rush a deal to beat the deadline, Lisa Albers with the Brown Deer Education Association said: "I think rushing sounds a little bit harsh. The whole thing was we would work together and come to a common agreement." However, the board adjourned saying it needed more time. "We intend to make sure that we look at the governor's repair bill, said board president Gary Williams, "whatever we propose will be consistent with the governor's repair bill."

Boycotts

Boycotts were implemented by opponents of Governor Walker's reforms by boycotting businesses that have made political contributions to Governor Walker. The activist said they want the companies to take a position on Walker's bill. Despite being part of the boycott, some of those businesses have not taken a position on the bill. One of the boycotted businesses, issued a statement that its employees contributed to both candidates in the last election. One labor union consortium consisting of the state's largest police and fire unions, along with some local teachers unions, urged their members to engage in what it characterized as "voluntary consumer activism."

There has been an effort by the *Wisconsin State Employees Union* to circulate threatening letters to businesses in southeast Wisconsin constraining them to support "workers' rights" by putting up a sign in their windows. If businesses fail to comply, the letter says, "Failure to do so will leave us no choice but (to) do a public boycott of your business. And sorry, neutral means 'no' to those who work for the largest employer in the area and are union members." One local business owner said "I was just disappointed; I didn't like the tone of the letter, To me, it bordered on strong-arm tactics." Another business owner put up a sign that read "We Support Workers Not Bully Tactics".

In an analysis of several concurrent public opinion polls, pollster Scott Rasmussen identified the source of seeming contradictions in the results. The results depended on the way the questions are worded. If the collective bargaining issue was worded in the context of balancing the state budget, Governor Walker does better. If the question is worded more narrowly, mentioning only the collective bargaining dispute, the unions fare better. A Pulse Opinion Research poll conducted of likely Wisconsin voters found that 56% support collective bargaining rights for public employees with 32% opposed. In the same poll, approval and disapproval for the bill was split at 50%–50% while 49% supported the protesters and 48% opposed them.

A poll of Wisconsin voters found that given a chance to vote in a rematch between Walker and his 2010 Democratic nominee , Walker would have lost 45%–52%. (In the actual election, Walker won 52–46 %.). The poll's analysis characterized the shift as the result of changing opinions due to the budget protests.

A poll released on March 9 showed that Americans were more likely to support limiting the collective bargaining powers of state employee unions to balance a state's budget (49%) than disapprove of such a measure (45%), while 6% had no opinion. 66% of Republicans approved of such a measure as did 51% of Independents. Only 31% of Democrats approved.

A poll released on March 11 showed that nationwide, Americans were more likely to give unions a negative word or phrase when describing them (38%) than a positive word or phrase (34%). 17% were neutral and 12% didn't know. Republicans were much more likely to say a negative term (58%) than Democrats (19%). Democrats were much more likely to say a positive term (49%) than Republicans (18%).

.Extreme Actions in Oklahoma and Norway

On April 19, 1995 an explosion blew apart a government building in Oklahoma City killing 168 people, 19 of them children and injuring close to 680 others. More than 300 buildings were affected.

Arrested for the bombing were Timothy McVeigh, who was convicted of planting the bomb, and Terry Nichols who helped design the bomb. Their convictions were assisted by testimony of people who knew them.

The main actor, Timothy McVeigh, tried to escape and when cited denied his guilt. Later when his conviction was assured and the evidence against him was concrete he made some statement about anger of a government siege incident in Waco and a place called Ruby Ridge where the government acted without patience to apprehend people who were wanted by the government. Timothy McVeigh was executed and Terry Nichols was given life in prison.

The second incident in this story took place in Norway the last week of July 2011. The actor was Anders Behring Breivik who began by setting off a car bomb in Oslo. From there he went to an island resort where hundreds of youths were attending a summer camp. He was dressed as a policeman and asked some of the people to gather for a talk. When the small crowd assembled he withdrew firearms and began killing them. By the time authorities were notified Breivik had killed 68 people. Once the authorities arrived Breivik surrendered without resistance. His trial will be forthcoming as this is written a week after his arrest.

The big difference in the two attacks is that the Oklahoma attack was made by a militant who did not want to be caught and defend his philosophy or motive for the attack. In the Norway massacre the actor not only surrendered by gave reasons for his action.

The Norway actor said that the attacks were "atrocious but necessary." He wanted publicity in order to warn Europe about Muslim and Marxist threats. Many of his victims were Muslim. Norway does not have the death penalty so we shall hear more from Anders Breivik in the future.

In breaking the law and publicly accepting responsibility the actor conveys a sense of disapproval or condemnation of certain policies or laws. By doing this, public attention is drawn to the law or policies by the events. Thereby the actor hopes to make changes in the policies or the law.

The laws governing this form of protest are designed as punishment for the action and as a deterrent to further action by others with the same intent. The laws are generally broad enough to condemn actions similar to the one in question.

After the assassination of President Kennedy, President Eisenhower said that practically anyone can be assassinated if the perpetrator is willing to put his life on the line. However, in our present legal system, few people, especially few rich people, ever have to put their life on the line. An assassin who is willing to stand up for a principle does not run away and send out messages through clandestine channels. There is certain leeway that must be given to assassins that make a statement and are willing to stand by that statement. Of course, it is my belief, that if you willingly take a human life you should sacrifice your own in return. However, an old adage has some merit, "He who fights and runs away, lives to fight another day."

The overt action of violence in the cases mentioned above is cause for supreme justice. But what justice can we get when we protest the rising price of gasoline by peacefully picketing the offices of gasoline companies or the policies of private banks. One may argue that we do not have to buy the gasoline or patronize the banks.

However, that is a moot point since gasoline prices and bank policies are coordinated and we do not actually have free enterprise and competitive pricing where they are concerned. Would burning the gasoline company office get more results than picketing? Is it worth going to jail to bring down gasoline prices or eliminating some bank gouging? If you burn the gasoline company office you might enforce a price change but you would not be in a position to enjoy the benefits of your sacrifice.

Terrorists vs Freedom Fighters

When various forms of revolution occur in a country it is usually a nation against the state. A nation is a large group of people having similar social, religious, and ethnic identities. A state is defined by its borders. The Kurdish nation exists in Turkey, Iraq and Iran. The Navajo Nation exists in the United States. At this time there are at least fifty nations trying to form their own state since most of them occupy a minority position in the state of their residence..

President Reagan referred to the anti-government forces in Nicaragua as *freedom fighters* and the anti-government forces in Israel as *terrorists*. Usually, our news media takes one side or the other and expresses this in their reports. The anti-government forces are labeled negatively as dissidents, guerillas, anarchists, separatists, terrorists, zealots, radicals, belligerents, etc.

Generally, revolutionary action centers on organized forcible resistance to the ruling authority. The actions can be militant, political, intimidating, or riotous. Whatever form it takes it is outside the realm of civil disobedience.

The term terrorist has serious negative connotations. It is often used by governments to include a wide range of actions. Most people who practice our concept of what we label terrorism do not use the term to describe their own actions. Governments often use the term terrorism when in many instances it is used to inflame rather than to be accurate. You have to be wary of the use of the term terrorist in designating you when you are a part of a political protest.

A political protest can have various degrees of disobedience performed by different factions within a movement. For instance, those engaged in protesting abortion have had silent vigils, peaceful protests, illegal interferences, as well as violence. The peaceful protesters almost always assert that they are against the violent methods of action in protesting. Taking the life of an abortion provider makes the slogan *pro-life* oxymoron. However, the illegal violent actions of the abortion protesters has had an effect on the system.

The militant protester can best be described as radical. He wants immediate change and is opposed to moderate forms of communication when describing his position. His needs of change are urgent. The militant protester does not want to take responsibility for his actions. He wants to run away and fight another day. He wants to hide in the hills, come down and keep up his barrage when it is convenient.

The militant or revolutionary protesters want a regime change and indeed in many areas of the world in past history have achieved that end. They keep their objectives obscure in order to confuse the masses who are being affected by their actions. They do not release numbers or any real information about themselves. The general aim of militant protesters, and in this case we will call them terrorists, is to generate insecurity and fear in the general population. In the United States some candidates for election use this insecurity and fear to their advantage. Who does this is so obvious that it needs no identification here. What is worrisome is that the general public buys into this and the people who use this approach have no conscience concerning it. .

Revolution and military action does not, as a rule, persuade governments to change established policies. Those changes have to come from within the government personnel rather than from the action of the belligerents. Those in power will generally try to hang onto power under any circumstance as well as any cost.

One of the aims of military action, or revolution, is to convince the government that they should cease to be the government. It would be good for the belligerents if all the people who will benefit by the change in government were in favor of the actions taken by the revolutionaries. It is possible to have revolutionary aims without engaging in military action. The case of Gandhi in India is an excellent example. His actions became so much a part of the general public's persona that the British simply gave up.

IV THE RIGHTS OF MAN AND THE USA PATRIOT ACT

The Rights of Man (and sometimes women)

U.S. Today and the French Revolutions

The Rights of Man was a book published by Thomas Paine in 1791. He argued political revolution was permissible when a government does not safeguard its people, their natural rights and their national interests. Since the time of Thomas Paine we have come to recognize many rights other than political.

Paine said human rights originate in Nature, thus, rights cannot be granted via political charter, because that implies that rights are legally revocable, hence, would be privileges rather than rights. For instance, a driver's license is a privilege.

"It is a perversion of terms to say that a charter gives rights. It operates by a contrary effect, that of taking rights away. Rights are inherently in all the inhabitants, but charters, by annulling those rights, in the majority, leave the right, by exclusion in the hands of a few. They consequently are instruments of injustice."

'The fact, therefore, must be that the individuals, themselves, each, in his own personal and sovereign right, entered into a compact with each other to produce a government: and this is the only mode in which governments have a right to arise, and the only principle on which they have a right to exist. Government's sole purpose is safeguarding the family and its inalienable rights, each societal institution that does not benefit the nation is illegitimate.'

The Rights of Man opposes the idea of hereditary government which is the belief that dictatorial government is necessary because of man's corrupt, essential nature.

At that time Paine's ideas were often opposed by those of Edmund Burke who said that true social stability arises if the nation's poor majority is governed by a minority of wealthy aristocrats, and that lawful inheritance of power should be the domain of the nation's elite social class, in this case he was talking about the nobility. In the present day he would be talking about those with wealth and political power.

The Rights of Man challenged Burke's assertion of the nobility's inherent hereditary wisdom. It said that a nation does not have a right to form a government for governing itself. Burke said that a government was "a contrivance of human wisdom." Paine argues that Government is a contrivance of man, and it follows that hereditary succession and hereditary rights to govern cannot compose a government because the wisdom to govern cannot be inherited.

The publication of Rights of Man caused such an uproar in England, remember they had a monarchy with power, that Thomas Paine was tried *in absentia* and convicted for crimes against the Crown, but was unavailable for hanging, having departed England for France.

Thomas Paine was not the only advocate of the rights of man or the only author of a work titled *Rights of Man*. The working-class radical, Thomas Spence. was among the first, in England, to use the phrase as a title. His 1775 lecture series were usually titled *The Rights of Man*, and his later *The Rights of Infants*, offer a sort of communist government alternative to Paine's democratic offering.

Other Rights Declarations - 1789

The Declaration of the Rights of Man and of the Citizen was designed to define the rights of the French Citizens. This was during the revolution. It defined the individual and collective rights of all the citizens as universal. The rights of man are valid at all times and in every place. It was a document ahead of its time but it did not address the practice of slavery nor did it concern itself with the status of women.

This declaration is heavily influenced by the Enlightenment principles of human rights. Previous to the time of the American and French Revolutions most philosophical writings and ideas were concerned with religion as the moral code of individuals and governments.

The Declaration lists a single set of individual and collective rights for all men. These rights are held to be written in stone (Ha) and held to be valid in all times and places. Men are born and remain free and equal in rights. Social distinctions may be founded only upon the general good. The role of government is to recognize and secure these rights. Government should be carried on by elected representatives.

These rights, at the time, were only awarded to men. The statement was a hope rather than a reality for the world did not seem ready for, at this time, what was in itself a revolution. It was a document related to the wars of the recent past where the abuses to humanity were shocking to say the least about it. Anyone espousing these rights were considered enemies of the monarchy and subject to persecution. The declaration was simply an ideal to which the French were pledged to attain for their future.

The Declaration begins with the natural rights of man which is liberty, property, security and resistance to oppression. It called for the destruction of aristocratic privileges by proclaiming the end of the aristocratic exemption from taxation, freedom and equal rights for all human beings. The terms "men and man" were used to refer to all human beings. All citizens should have access to public office and take part in the legislative process. Arbitrary arrests were outlawed.

The social equality of citizens was a tenet. "All citizens, equal in the eyes of the law, are equally admissible to all public dignities, places and employments according to their capacity and without distinction other than that of their virtues and their talents." This was to eliminate the special rights of the nobility and the clergy who dominated appointments in the military and government offices.

Some of the declaration rights were stated. Among them were the aim of all political association is the preservation of the natural rights of man. These rights are liberty, property, security and resistance to oppression.

The principle of all sovereignty resides essentially in the nation. No group or individual may exercise any authority which does not proceed directly from the nation and its laws.

Liberty consists in the freedom to do everything which injures no one else. The natural rights of the individual has no limits except those which assure to the other members of society the enjoyment of the same rights. The limits of this freedom can only be determined by law. Law can only prohibit such actions as are harmful to society. Nothing may be prevented which is not forbidden by law. No one will be forced to do anything not approved for by the law.

The Law is the expression of the general will. Every citizen has a right to participate personally in its foundation. It must be the same for all, whether it protects or punishes. All citizens, being equal in the eyes of the law are equally eligible to all dignities and to all public positions and occupations, according to their abilities, and without distinction except that of their virtues and talents.

No person shall be accused, arrested, or imprisoned except in the cases and according to the forms prescribed by law. Any one soliciting, transmitting, executing, or causing to be executed, any arbitrary order, shall be punished. But any citizen summoned or arrested in virtue of the law shall submit without delay, as resistance constitutes an offense.

The law shall provide for such punishments only as are strictly and obviously necessary, and no one shall suffer punishment except it be legally inflicted in virtue of a law passed and promulgated before the commission of the offense.

As all persons are held innocent until they shall have been declared guilty, if arrest shall be deemed indispensable, all harshness not essential to the securing of the prisoner's person shall be severely repressed by law.

No one shall be disquieted on account of his opinions, including his religious views, provided their manifestation does not disturb the public order established by law. The free communication of ideas and opinions is one of the most precious of the rights of man. Every citizen may, accordingly, speak, write, and print with freedom, but shall be responsible for such abuses of this freedom as shall be defined by law.

The security of the rights of man and of the citizen requires public military forces. These forces are, therefore, established for the good of all and not for the personal advantage of those to whom they shall be entrusted.

A common contribution is essential for the maintenance of the public forces and for the cost of administration. **This should be equitably distributed among all the citizens in proportion to their means.**

All the citizens have a right to decide, either personally or by their representatives, as to the necessity of the public contribution; to grant this freely; to know to what uses it is put; and to fix the proportion, the mode of assessment and of collection and the duration of the taxes.

Society has the right to require of every public agent an account of his administration.

A society in which the observance of the law is not assured, nor the separation of powers defined, has no constitution at all. Since property is an inviolable and sacred right, no one shall be deprived thereof except where public necessity, legally determined, shall clearly demand it, and then only on condition that the owner shall have been previously and equitably indemnified.

Some Twists to the Declaration

As mentioned previously, women and slaves, were not specifically mentioned in these rights. The women in the French Revolution were active in the assemblies. It was written that one woman said "he who votes against the right of another, whatever the religion, color or sex of that other has henceforth abjured his own rights."

Later a Declaration of the Rights of Woman and the female Citizen was enacted. Women in America did not get the right to vote until a hundred years after this declaration. The declaration states "This declaration will only take effect when all women become fully aware of their deplorable condition, and of the rights they have lost in society.

The USA PATRIOT ACT

Not many know that the USA PATRIOT ACT is an acronym for Uniting and Strengthening America by Providing Appropriate Tools Required to Intercept and Obstruct Terrorism Act. It was signed into law on 26 October 2001. The Act was a response to the terrorist attacks on September 11 of that year. The Act gave law enforcement agencies almost unlimited powers to search telephone, email, medical records, financial records, regulate financial transactions with foreign entities and gave officials the right to detain and deport immigrants suspected of terrorist related acts. The law expanded the definition of terrorism to include domestic terrorism. (My opinion) The domestic terrorism provision enables law enforcement to legally tap anyone's communication avenues with impunity.

It is doubtful that more than a handful of people have read the Act in its entirety. It was passed without much debate and immediately signed into law by President Bush II. Probably the only people that have read the Act are those who wrote it and they probably only read the portion that they wrote. Slowly, its provisions are being released to the public by special interest groups who were concerned with their own bailiwick.

My West Virginia man Fred has always maintained that almost any law enacted by Congress takes away some of our freedom. At times, he could also be described as a "right wing" zealot. With the Patriot Act, I had him in my power and wrote to him that our domestic freedoms were at stake here and the threat of terrorism was not as great as the Bush people indicated. The terrorists had expended their resources in that September 11 attack.

Fred wrote back, "The Patriot Act does not bother me since I have nothing to hide." After several more exchanges of opinions he finally wrote that he had made a mistake on the Patriot Act and it needed "appended in its operations of domestic nature."

Anything connected with the investigations of the Act was classified information and so the general public was not able to judge what was going on. This reminded me of the time President Lyndon Johnson spoke at Syracuse University when I was a student there. He had just announced his response to the Gulf of Tonkin incident. He couldn't give us any information concerning his actions because the information he had was classified. Any rational person realizes that much of the information that is "Classified" is to protect the classifier rather than the country. So it is with the USA Patriot Act.

We are assured that the Patriot Act has done more than get President G. W. Bush elected to a second term. But, we will not know if this is true since most of the material is classified. Some of this trickles out such as the incident outside of Buffalo New York where five Muslims were arrested for alleged plots of terrorism.

It is difficult not to think of Hitler's move in 1933 to annihilate his opposition by killing and imprisoning them and making a public statement that he had acted to prevent a takeover of the government by hostile forces. Actually, he was the one that took over the government with this abuse of power.

Anyway, President Barack Obama signed a four year extension of the Act on 26 May 2011 where it concerns searches of business records, roving wire taps and surveillance of individuals suspected of terrorist related activities not linked to terrorist groups.

Some critics of the Act believed it was passed with not enough debate. It was hurried through the process with little change. The enormous document surely had many provisions that needed debate. However, the emergency of the situation might have justified this haste. A debate would have slowed down the legislation and prevented the FBI from acting quickly. The FBI is not exactly known for always employing legal methods to justify its ends.

Most of what we know about the Act comes to us in a round-about way. Advocates play upon our fears of terrorism and opponents play on our fears of government intimidation. The law gives the FBI a blank check to violate the communications privacy of innocent Americans. It is difficult to understand this attitude since there is nothing in my communications that would embarrass me if it was made public. However, many persons would be upset if their private communications were intercepted. The changing technologies of communication almost require the government authorities in charge of our security to have some ability to investigate and counteract terrorists who use modern techniques of communication. In the old days, they could tap telephones. Now with cell phones and other sophisticated communication devices it is a challenge to keep track of would-be terrorists. Thus, the roving wire-taps might be justified.

It used to be that a wiretap required a court order, but now with voice mail the lack of notice almost has to be violated. One problem was that if the FBI listened to voice mail illegally, according to the Fourth Amendment, it couldn't use the information to obtain a conviction. The Act made the interception of voice mail legal. There was a big flap a few years ago when phone companies began giving the government their files with the information of who called whom and when. The individual will not know if they are under surveillance since only the phone company will receive a warrant if one is issued and not the individual in question.

The Act has come under revision by simple restraint of activities of the law enforcement authority. The Fourth Amendment has caused them to draw back on some of their activities. Some feel it is necessary for swift action because a delay may give a terrorist a chance to warn his fellow terrorists that such a search was underway.

In 2004, FBI agents used this provision to search and secretly examine the home of one Brandon Mayfield, who was wrongfully jailed for two weeks on suspicion of involvement in the Madrid Train bombings. While the U.S. Government **did** publicly apologize to Mayfield and his family, Mayfield took it further through the courts. On September 26, 2007, judge Ann Aiken found the law was, in fact, unconstitutional as the search was an unreasonable imposition on Mayfield and thus violated the Fourth Amendment.

The Act also is criticized because it prohibits Americans from association with groups that have been deemed hostile to the United States. For instance, there are many of our citizens working with these groups on a humanitarian basis, such as children orphaned when their parents have been annihilated in conflicts such as between Israel and its enemies, which are by extension our enemies. The Act is worded in such a way that it is almost impossible for a humanitarian to know whether they are breaking the law or not. The First Amendment covers this right of American citizens.

In its November 2005 issue *Business Week* reported that the FBI had obtained one million financial, credit, employment, and in some cases, health records from the customers of targeted businesses in Las Vegas. Selected businesses included casinos, storage warehouses and car rental agencies. The individual involved in these searches was unaware of the search and therefore cannot challenge the legality of the search in court.

The Library Controversy

Part of the Act permitted the FBI to access library records to see who was reading, I suppose, controversial literature. When I read about this provision I thought about the time I was in the Army and stationed in Germany during the Cold War and had a copy of Das Capital by Karl Marx in my locker. When the captain who was inspecting our rooms went through my books and discovered the book he tried to engage me in debate about it, while I was at attention. I had to admit that I could not read it since it made little sense to me. He was pacified. I also told him that we should all wish to know what our enemy was thinking and besides I bought the book at the PX.

Here is some of what happened to the library provision according to Wikepedia. Section 215 allows the FBI to apply for an order to produce materials that assist in an investigation undertaken to protect against international terrorism or clandestine intelligence activities. Among the "tangible things" that could be targeted, it includes "books, records, papers, documents, and other items". Supporters of the provision point out that these records are held by third parties, and therefore are exempt from a citizen's reasonable expectations of privacy and also maintain that the FBI has not abused the provision.

As proof, then Attorney General John Ashcroft released information in 2003 that showed that section 215 orders had never been used. However, despite protestations to the contrary, the American Library Association strongly objected to the provision, believing that library records are fundamentally different from ordinary business records, and that the provision would have a chilling effect on free speech... They urged librarians to seek legal advice before complying with a search order and advised their members to only keeping records for as long as was legally needed. Consequently, reports started filtering in that librarians were shredding records to avoid having to comply with such orders.

In 2005, Library Connection, a nonprofit consortium of 27 libraries in Connecticut, received a National Security Letter (NSL) from the FBI, along with its accompanying perpetual gag order, demanding library patrons' records. George Christian, executive director of

Library Connection, and three members of the executive committee of the board engaged the ACLU to file suit to challenge the constitutional validity of the NSL. Because Section 505 of the USA PATRIOT Act, which authorizes the FBI to demand records without prior court approval, also forbids, or gags, anyone who receives an NSL from telling anyone else about receiving it, they also challenged the validity of the gag order. For almost a year the ACLU fought to lift the gag order, challenging the government's power under Section 505 to silence four citizens who wished to contribute to public debate on the PATRIOT Act. In May 2006, the government finally gave up its legal battle to maintain the gag order.

My observation is that with internet access libraries are going the way of typewriters, the slide rule and adding machines.

Another provision of the Act permits an indefinite detention of any alien believed to be associated with terrorism or suspected of this mind-set. Challengers say the Act deprives basic rights of immigrants to America and its resources. The critics have said that this provision of the Act allows the Attorney General to detain persons based on mere suspicion. The ACLU has accused the Act of giving the Attorney General "unprecedented new power to determine the fate of immigrants... Worse, if the foreigners do not have a country that will accept them, they can be detained indefinitely without trial."

A further controversial provision of the Act involves gathering information from files that have crossed the border between the United States and Canada. Many companies outsource their activities across this border. Many Canadian groups have filed protests with the United States. "What's wrong with the Cannucks, don't they realize there's a war on?"

V HUMAN RIGHTS

London, England August 2011

There were two days of vandalism, looting and melee beginning August 8 in London. Once the success of the looters in London was made public the action spread to other cities via internet, television and cell phone. Thirty five London police officers were injured before 16,000 special police were able to quell the riots and establish order.

Many of the satellite cities of London became the scene of groups of young people, mostly young men, simply smashing store windows and taking the contents on display.

The following police reports appeared on the internet. -Three officers injured after being hit by a vehicle in Chingford Mount, Waltham Forest, at about 00:45 BST - More than 30 youths vandalizing and looting a number of shops in Walthamstow and Waltham Forest - Vandalism carried out by about 50 youths in Oxford Circus, central London - A police vehicle being attacked in Islington, north London - A shop on the King's Road in Chelsea damaged - A Tesco store in Ponders End being attacked and items stolen

The rioting lasted the best part of two days when the police gained absolute control of the situation. More than seven hundred people were arrested. The local courts remained open around the clock processing those brought in as law breakers.\

Not all the rioters were young men. The press release identified an eleven year old boy, a teenage ballerina and a student from a prosperous family. Two young women had taken television sets. One of them gave herself up as her conscience bothered her. The other was turned in by her parents who saw her rioting on television. The mayor of London said that it was "fitting, that significant sentences were being handed down" to those immediately pleading guilty.

Comment: These riots were simply vandalism spurred on by the moment and the participants were looking for excitement rather than protesting some injustice of the system under which they were living.

Damascus, Syria 2011

The following is modified from several articles, mainly from Wikipedia.

The **2011 Syrian uprising** is an ongoing internal conflict, occurring in Syria since March 2011. Protests began on 26 January 2011, and escalated to an uprising by 15 March 2011. The demands of protesters include for President Bashar al Assad to step down, for the ruling Baath Party to allow the existence of competitive parties, to end extrajudicial killings and torture, equal rights for Syria's ethnic and religious groups, and broad political freedoms, such as freedom of press, speech and assembly. Like the revolutionary movements in Tunisia and Egypt it has taken the form of protests of various types, including marches and hunger strikes as well as vandalism of government property and rioting of shops, in a sustained campaign of civil resistance. Some Islamic groups in the Syrian north have allegedly taken advantage of protests to launch attacks against the government. There have also been some reported instances of sectarian clashes between the majority Sunni population and Syrians loyal to the regime.

More than 2,000 protesters have been killed, many more injured, and thousands detained, while the Syrian government says armed Islamist elements in the country are responsible for the civilian casualties and the killing of more than 340 members of the security forces.

As protests continued, the Syrian government used tanks and snipers to force people off the streets. Water and electricity were shut off and security forces began confiscating flour and food in particularly restive areas.

Activists, fleeing civilians, and soldiers who defected claimed that soldiers who refuse to fire on civilians are executed by the Syrian Army. The Syrian government has denied the reports of defections and blamed "armed gangs" for causing trouble.

News August 14, 2011 Syrian Forces Kill Three

Associated Press Release – Syrian tanks, security agents and pro-regime gunmen fanned out into the streets of two towns to root out protesters demanding the ouster of President Bashar Assad in a sweep Saturday that killed at least three people.

Later in the day, shooting and explosions were heard in another neighborhood, Slaibeh, according to the Observatory For Human Rights and the Local Coordination Committees, an activist group that documents protests in Syria. Two people were killed in the shooting.

Follow up side bar – The U.S. Issued new penalties against Syria last week, and Secretary of State, Hillary Rodham Clinton has called for a global trade embargo on oil and gas from the Middle East nation.--- Rights groups said at least 1,700 civilians have been killed in the violent crackdown.

In order to understand the activity in Syria we go back to the premise that we are programmed for survival and all our actions are somehow tied into this programming. Why should not President Assad use force against and kill his enemies. They want to kill him and do away with him in some manner in order that they may have a bigger share of the resources. If they can get enough supporters and keep together they will probably have success in their endeavor. They will be aided in their efforts by the United States, Great Britain and a few Mid East countries who probably have a religious ax to grind. This was successful in removing Gaddafi in Libya so why not use it to get Assad in Syria?

In any revolution the power that is the target of the revolution, will not yield any of that power unless absolutely forced to do so. This is true in the United States, as well as in Syria.

One of the mistakes some revolutionaries make is to leave a beaten enemy still standing. Successful revolutionaries are those that kill their targets if they can get at them. Those revolutionaries who have done so in the past have had a longer span of rule than those who did not. Eventually they transfer toward democracy because they have become aged and feeble, unless they have like minded youthful successors. Cuba is a good example of what has just been written.

What was your reaction to the statement that 1,700 people were killed? Did the number sink in? Stalin said that if you kill a person that is a tragedy, but if you kill two thousand, that is a statistic. What do the number of deaths have to say to us in our mind? If one of the over four thousand deaths in our war in Iraq is not connected to you how does the number four thousand affect you concerning American deaths? Is it a tragedy or is it a statistic?

One of the running arguments I have with my NRA friend Fred concerns a government order for troops to fire on civilians. Fred believes the members of the military would not fire on their own citizens. I point out the Kent State fiasco. Fred backs off a little. My opinion is that a government order to fire on civilians would be obeyed, especially if the soldiers were from a different area other than the one where the action was in progress. .

Human Rights – An old saying "Might makes right"

All men are created equal ...entitled to "life, liberty and the pursuit of happiness." This was written by my favorite American of the Revolution. Those words were written by a man who owned a large number of black slaves at the time he wrote it. His words would have true meaning if he thought of black people as not being human. But, he treated his slaves as human beings and even cohabited with some of them.

Not so in the circles of William Bartram whose activities are published in his memoirs and other books about his and his father's lives. At one time William was the owner of seven black slaves. A friend of his wrote about "poor" William "here he is living in desolation with no human beings to talk to." There is no doubt of that writer's mindset.

What are human rights and who are the advocates of human rights and for whom do they advocate? One old saying is "your rights stop where my nose begins."

Is the following a fair statement? If we in power grant rights to others then we give up some of our own rights and power. By granting more rights we limit the power we have over people thus we diminish some of the value of the resources we control. That is an abstract thought and one might say the dilution of value is insignificant. That may be true, but will the challenger admit that giving more rights by those in power to others is a decrease in the resources of those holding the power. Here, we look at the right as a resource since it would have value that can be transferred in some fashion to finance.

Most humans would probably want other humans to have the rights of life, liberty and the pursuit of happiness, especially if they don't have to yield any of that which belong to them by advocating these rights to others. Isn't everyone a human rights advocate?

Human rights are basic rights and freedoms all people are entitled to according to being born human. Sometimes the divisions of humanity have to be identified as one of the divisions is denied human rights and have been denied in the past. These divisions include sex, ethnic origins, religion, language and nationality. These rights may exist as natural rights but the only assurance we have of getting them is by legislation and enforcement of the legislation. We may get these rights simply because of our position in a society and no legislation is necessary toward that end. .

Most historians agree that the concept of human rights around the world was initiated after World War II. For instance, in the United States, women did not have the right to vote during World War I. But then again, is the right to vote one of the human rights of the discussion?

The Universal Declaration of Human Rights adopted in Paris by the United Nations General Assembly in 1948 was a statement that the world should accept and encourage. The philosophy of human rights was espoused by many philosophers of the eighteenth century which can be argued to have given rise to the American and French Revolutions.

Probably the Holocaust was the main influence on creating The Declaration of Human Rights in 1948. The attitude of the Soviet Union, that was militantly denying human rights during that time, would make an interesting study. An ardent protester in the United States in 1948 might end up in prison but a protester in the Soviet Union more often than not ended up at the morgue.

It was the protester that put human rights in the conscience of America. Illegal barriers to legal activism and political discourse were slowly broken down. Early human rights movements around the world usually involved totalitarianism. As totalitarian regimes continue to collapse the human rights movements in the world arena have shifted to social and economic development as well as humanitarian considerations.

We can all find agreement in arguments for human rights on the basis of politics and security from government abuse, but are things like decent medical care, housing and food also human rights? Do we grant these benefits to people who do not work or produce some benefit to society. We do in the United States and here a controversy develops as to whether or not human rights should be earned rather than freely given. Have human rights become part of social expectation?

Should the extension and protection of human rights be established on a code of moral behavior? If you don't do such and such, you don't get such and such. Should religious practices be a part of establishing human rights? If we have to kill the infidels we certainly don't give much value to their human rights.

Human rights are established by rules of order accepted from a legitimate authority in exchange for security and possibly economic advantage. Granting of human rights by an authority is a social contract.

The two theories that dominate contemporary human rights discussion are the interest theory and the will theory. *Interest* theory argues that the principal function of human rights is to protect and promote certain essential human interests, while *will* theory attempts to establish the validity of human rights based on the unique human capacity for freedom. The strong claims made by human rights to universality have led to persistent criticism.

HYPERLINK ""

Human rights can be classified and organized in a number of different ways, an international level the most common categorization of human rights has been to split them into civil and political rights. There are also divisions of social, economic and cultural rights. It may be argued that these rights can only be had in combination with each other. This is true because without civil and political rights the public cannot assert their economic, social and cultural rights. Similarly, without livelihoods and a working society, the public cannot assert or make use of civil or political rights

The Vienna Declaration of Human Rights of 1993 states that All human rights are universal, indivisible and interdependent and related. The international community must treat human rights globally in a fair and equal manner, on the same footing, and with the same emphasis. This statement was again endorsed at the 2005 World Summit in New York.

Some countries have given priority to civil and political rights at the expense of economic and social rights such as health care. In the United States we have health care but it comes at a high cost and therefore we cannot claim it to be a human right in our culture. In most of Europe universal health care is a right. In some countries such as the "Stans" of central Asia there is a granting of economic and cultural rights but no civil and political rights.

Opponents of the indivisibility of human rights argue that economic, social and cultural rights are fundamentally different from civil and political rights and require completely different approaches. Economic, social and cultural rights are argued to be philosophical and subject to the whims of a changing society.

There is no unanimous opinion on what should and shouldn't be provided as a right. And if some such right as healthcare is acknowledged and provided is there some manner of measurement that assures us that it is adequate.

There is a large number of people in the United States who believe that healthcare should not be the concern of the government. This attitude is usually presented by people who have adequate healthcare at their disposal. They see themselves as having earned their way in life and have secured adequate health care for themselves and family. They do not see the healthcare issue as one of social and economic disadvantage.

We return to the hope that everyone is entitled to and has life, liberty and the pursuit of happiness. We also have to consider that they may also be entitled to decent housing, a good paying job, security in their person and in their health and that they maintain these after their working days have ended.

Martial Law

When the social protesting gets to unmanageable proportions Martial Law may be put in force. This is the imposition of military rule by military authorities over designated regions on an emergency basis and is usually only temporary when the civilian government or civilian authorities fail to function effectively (e.g., maintain order and security, and provide essential services). When there are extensive riots and protests, or when the disobedience of the law becomes widespread, then martial law may be necessary. In most cases, military groups are deployed to quiet the crowds and to secure government buildings. They are also deployed at key or sensitive locations, and to maintain order.

With Martial Law, military personnel replace civil authorities and perform most of their functions. The constitution of the country could be suspended. The highest ranking military officer would take over as the leader, therefore removing all power from the previous executive, legislative and judicial branches of government.

Martial Law has often been used to suppress political opposition, to stabilize insurrections or sometimes to jump-the-gun on proposed organized protesting by declaring a state of emergency..

Martial law has also been imposed during conflicts and in cases of occupations, where the absence of any other civil government provides for an unstable population. Examples of this form of military rule include post reconstruction in Germany and Japan.

Typically, the imposition of martial law accompanies the suspension of civil liberties and the application or extension of military law to civilians. Civilians defying martial law may be subjected to many punishments. In cases of curfew a shoot-to-kill order is often given.

Is Protesting A Moral Right?

Back in the 1960s when marijuana use had clouded peoples thoughts there was a phenomena of panic about it. The clouding was not of the mind of those who used marijuana but in the minds of those who saw it as a threat to the public in general. A series of punitive legislation against buyers and sellers of the product were enacted throughout the country. Many of these are still on the books today.

One of the techniques used by police to apprehend criminals is to "pull them over" on the pretext of driving under the influence or safety violations of the vehicles. In the use of marijuana a profile of users and sellers was developed.

At that time, mid 1960's, any man driving a van, especially a beat up van and sporting long hair and a beard could not drive across the Pennsylvania Turnpike without being stopped more than once by the state troopers. This was usually accompanied by illegal searches of the van and the people in it. Sometimes violence erupted.

As a result of many protests and law suits this practice was diminished but not eliminated altogether. It was a victory of protest.

Today we have the Patriot Act which is an invasion of privacy on a grand scale. Few statistics are available on the subject as to its accomplishment.

Do people have a right to civil disobedience? That is, do people have a legal right as well as a moral right to protest legislation or assumed legislation? We must assume they do and this right should not be curtailed unless perhaps the protest detracts from the civil liberties and personal safety of others. The protest is justified when there is a clear injustice occurring. It is justified especially when other people or groups also recognize that injustice is occurring. And maybe, the protest is the needed result after all legal means of discussion and debate have been fruitless.

The right to protest is a question of moral right. If a protest is morally right is there a protest that is morally wrong? Morality is a human invention and as such we can label it as good or bad according to our perceptions and consciences. **We cannot restrict protests only to those that society deems to be morally right.** However, we must be willing to accept responsibility for what results from our actions whether morally right or wrong.

If a protest is legal and morally correct then any interference with that protest would be morally and legally wrong. So, if we have a right to political protest we can do that only if our actions are within the framework of recognized rights. We are talking about protesting in a somewhat just society. **The legal aspect of one's protest does not necessarily depend on the validity of one's cause.** Only in a just society does a person possess a legitimate right to protest. When a person's rights are violated by law they have a right to disregard the offending law and take the consequences of that disregard. Protesting is a moral right which is generally not recognized by law in many societies. **In a just society protesting is a right recognized by law. .**

If we organize a protest and our actions are detrimental to the welfare of other people not involved in our protest then we must not criticize the government for outlawing such action. However, it is possible that the protestors view might have won out had the protester given more time to discussion and debate. Patience is a virtue that is often rewarded.

In this sense we have a feeling that time is running out as our legislators are side-tracked by personal vendettas and prejudices rather than attacking the problems of our society.

It must be repeated that when a government rejects pubic discussions of a situation and the media does not give the problem a fair coverage then the defenders of the unpopular view must move to action and even employ bizarre or sensational methods to gain attention and perhaps effect a change.

Conscience

We can protest a law by not obeying it on the basis of conscience. Thus we have had conscientious objectors to the military draft. By making the military voluntary a lot of problems were solved, but others created. Draft dodging and conscientious objection were eliminated from legal prosecution. In order to encourage military enlistment large increases in military salaries were given. One severe problem that still exists is how to get people of high education and intelligence to enlist in the military. Not that all volunteers are dummies, after all, they are all high school graduates. But it takes a special type of intelligence to operate much of the highly technical weapons we have developed for today's arsenal. It may be a rumor but I read of a situation where field commanders in Afghanistan had to abandon highly sophisticated weapons because there was no one that knew how to operate them effectively.

When protests start to hit at the heart of legislation held dear by many legislators then a tendency to safeguard that legislation may exist and means to squelch the protests engaged. As a protestor we must retain dignity and many governments thwart the protest by taking away dignity with such actions as using water hoses, tear gas and attack dogs. Is a man dressed in bum clothes and unkempt hair treated with dignity during his protest. I don't think so. A well dressed demonstrator will receive more respect, not only from the authorities and the media, but from the general public than a slovenly one, even though their arguments may be equally valid.

The right to assemble and protest should be guarded and protected by the government if all legal obligations to hold the protest or assembly are fulfilled. **The right of people to protest their government should be honored, encouraged and insured by that government**

If a law has been broken during an act of civil disobedience then we assume an arrest should be made. Either the authority or the police on hand must make a judgment on that issue. Sometimes it is best to ignore the violation and not give some "crazy" a chance to spout off. However, this might spur the "crazy" into other actions that might be intolerable or detrimental to social stability.

Once the arrest has been made then a speedy trial is necessary, at least in our country. It is up to a judge or a jury to decide guilt or innocence and if it is guilt then up to a judge to decide how much to punish. Often the decision of a judge has resulted in further protesting and civil disobedience.

We cannot ignore the fact that civil disobedience should be punished when the law has been broken in a "just" society. And we assume our American society is "just," or nearly so. Therefore, let us proceed and present theories even if we have not identified the originators of those theories.

Some people look upon punishment as an evil in itself. They believe that punishment should only be effected if some greater evil should arise by not punishing.

Punishment is often considered as a deterrent to further crime. It seems to encourage the thinking that people who commit a specific crime will repeat that crime unless they were punished in some manner. However, the theory includes the idea that punishment of a crime will deter other people from committing that same crime.

A problem with punishment is in deciding the degree of punishment necessary to justify the aims of punishment. How much punishment does a person deserve and should they get what they deserve? Should a person involved because of gullibility receive the same penalty as one who knew precisely the extent of the crime. In the old west, as Gus said to Jake, "If you ride with them, you die with them." We must realize though, that we are not in the old west.

Not too long ago there was a local man involved in a brutal beating of another man who was a stranger to the beater. The lawyer of the offender was interviewed on television saying that the beater was sorry

for his actions, it was a spur of the moment thing, he is really remorseful and also he has been taking Bible classes while incarcerated and awaiting trial. Religion and patriotism are cloaks that have been used to shield many a bad actor. In the case of punishment the state is obligated to confirm its condemnation of the Acton with the idea that punishment would lead to reformation of the criminal activity. Perhaps condemnation is enough of a punishment. A repentant criminal is usually treated with more leniency than one who is not. Therefore it is in the criminal's best interest to be openly repentant before the jury announces its verdict, since the granting of mercy is a human trait, or is it a human failure.

What does all that have to do with protesting. If the protest adds criminality to it then the protestors must have some strategy concerning eventually punishment. Will they plead ignorance of the severity of their actions? Will they argue their intent was not to harm" Will they plead for mercy? "Plead" is an inflammatory word, so would they "solicit" mercy?

As to punishment of a protest, probably a greater punishment than that of a non-protestor committing the same act should be enforced if deterrent is to be effected. Most protesters, I believe, are not deterred by standard punishments but that does not mean their punishment should match that of a career criminal.

We would expect an "idealistic" protestor, that does not harm anyone, to be treated leniently. But the element of fairness to others who committed the same act would in itself be subject to protest. Trespassing to protest a farmers use of pesticides by burning them is not the same as stealing the farmers chickens, that is in a moral sense. Burning the pesticide might be morally justified while stealing is usually not morally justified. What if the chicken thief was only trying to feed his family? However, society decides what is moral and immoral in its eyes. Moral arguments could be based on motivation, type of action and justification. When these are considered is not a conscientious protest less serious than a common criminal act? Again we are considering an illegal act and making decisions according to the rule of law. Trespassing and damage to property are the charges for the above acts. Which one does society consider to be the least offensive to its structure?

If Fred is arrested for stealing chickens in Georgia nobody in Pennsylvania will hear of it. But, if Fred incinerates a tank load of pesticides it will probably be national news.

VI THE TAX DILEMMA

A study of 342 US protests against corporations covered by the New York Times newspaper in the period 1962 and 1990 showed that such public activities usually had an impact on the company's publicly-traded price. The most intriguing aspect of the study findings is that what mattered most was not the number of protest participants, but the amount of media coverage the event received. Stock prices fell an average of one-tenth of a percent for every paragraph printed about the event.

Warren Buffet entered his opinion into the public domain in a New York Times op-ed piece on 8 August 2011. He said he would immediately raise tax rates on households with taxable income of more than one million dollars and he would add an additional increase for those making ten million dollars or more. He also recommended that the 12 members of Congress charged with devising a deficit-cutting plan leave rates for 99.7 percent of taxpayers unchanged. "My friends and I have been coddled long enough by a billionaire friendly Congress." and "It's time for our government to get serious about shared sacrifice."

It didn't take long for some opposition to form. Republicans responded with "tweets" questioning Buffet's sincerity. Why were they all Republicans and no Democrats since Buffet didn't accuse any political party, just Congress, in his statements?

"For tax raising advocates like Warren Buffet, I am sure Treasury would take a voluntary payment for deficit reduction." said Senator John Cornyn, a Texas Republican.

"If Warren Buffet wants to pay more taxes and send more of his money to Washington, why doesn't he just do it?" tweeted the spokesman for Representative Eric Cantor, Republican from West Virginia who has led the cause against tax increases.

Buffet said his comments were aimed at the "super twelve" committee entrusted with the job of cutting the deficit. He rejected the claim that raising taxes to cut the U.S. Deficit will kill jobs. He said the country had higher taxes between 1980 and 2000 and "nearly 40 million jobs were added."

Mike Brownfield of the conservative think tank Heritage Foundation was quoted as saying, "A billionaire calling for more taxes might make great political theater but there's more to the story than Buffett.would have you believe."

On The Subject of Federal Taxes

The tax system of a country has been one of the major factors in a revolution within that country.. We point with pride to the Tea Tax revolt in American history when the English citizens, dressed as Native Americans, threw bundles of cargo into the bay. We, in the United States, are certainly on the brink of a revolution concerning our **incomprehensible tax laws** and its structure, not to mention its present preferential treatment of the rich and privileged.

Fred

My friend Fred lives in a rural area of West Virginia and writes me a letter twice a week and I respond to him twice a week. We have been doing this for about thirty years. In almost all of Fred's letters he makes some reference to taxes. He will send a news clipping about welfare fraud and write in the margin "send more tax money."

Fred will send me a copy of his grocery bill and with arrows point to the taxes on food and newspapers. He will also make a notation beside a dollar can of tuna such as, "was 79 cents a year ago – govt. says no inflation, ha ha."

Fred is marginally employed at this time. And he lives alone. He is a champion of tax cuts although his income is such that he pays no income tax. He was a big supporter of Bush II's "tax cuts for the rich." Fred also supported the idea of privatizing social security.

Fred is not yet available for social security and assumes it will be defunct when he is eligible in four years. I can't wait until Fred discovers he has to pay taxes on his social security income. He also has no health insurance but was militantly opposed to "Obama Care."

When Fred was gainfully employed for about twenty years he was paying around ten grand in income tax a year on his earnings. He is sitting back on his ridge in West Virginia waiting a call from some tax group to march on his state capital or on Washington.

Corporations and Taxes

With the Supreme Court decision allowing corporations to contribute freely to political campaigns, as well as giving them the ability to fund interest groups for political advertising, the scenario for a wild west shoot out is all set.

Corporation taxes are set at thirty five percent but no corporation ever pays anywhere near that amount. Boeing paid four and a half percent over a five year period. Southwest Airlines paid six point three percent during that same period.

Samuel King of the Greenlining Institute is quoted in *The Week,* September 2, 2011 on which this article is based said, "It is unpatriotic, its unfair, and we can't afford it. ..Congress is looking to cut the deficit by slashing Medicare, Social Security, food safety, education, and health without collecting another dime from these wealthy companies."

Companies avoid paying the full tax by using accounting gimmicks and tax shelters created by lobbyists and lawyers. One strategy is to shift jobs, operations and profits to overseas subsidiaries in low tax countries.

Company executives have said that they would be willing to bring these jobs back home if the home taxes were more reasonable. However, this sort of amnesty was tried in 2004 and the three hundred billion dollars that came back was not spent on creating jobs, it was used to buy more stock and give shareholder dividend payments.

General Electric has a staff of 975 lawyers working for them and their job is to figure out how to lower their taxes and they have successfully done so since they had profits of fourteen point two billion dollars in 2010 and paid less than one percent in federal taxes.

These loopholes amount to over a hundred billion dollars a year in lost revenue. On the one hand the corporations argue that the "high" tax rates force them to move business overseas and forces them to create and use the loopholes they have created by buying congressmen. On the other hand the country needs more revenue and closing these loopholes would be one way of getting it.

Tax Resistance

Nobody likes to see their income diminished by taxation but thinking people realize that taxes are necessary for the operation of government and are usually willing to pay them without protest. But, there are facets of government expenditure which are questionable and using tax money on these expenditures is a source of much discontent to some people. At this time there are militant protesters who decry the federal expenditures on war, abortion, welfare and education. Many of these protestors are in the spotlight from time to time. Withholding taxes with a note about the particular protest usually has the tax resistor heading for the courthouse, sometimes in handcuffs.

Before women got the right to vote in this country there were many tax resisters in the suffrage movement. There are young people today who claim the right to vote on the basis that they do pay taxes and they should have the privilege of input concerning who will represent them. Forget it kid.

There are also complaints concerning the method of collecting taxes. The genius who came up with the idea of withholding taxes from payrolls was worthy of the Liberty Medal which is so freely handed out these days.

Resistance to paying taxes could be used to overthrow the taxing system. If everyone refused to fill out the 1040 form our courts would be overwhelmed with business as would our prisons. Certainly, if a large group of citizens refused to pay taxes and demand their day in court it would make a statement that could not be ignored by our legislators. Don't count on it. They would argue for patience.

The federal and state governments depend on consent of the citizens in the nature of taxation and therefore the welfare if the state is at stake when the consent is not provided by the citizens. Withholding taxes from the government would destabilize it and cause its downfall. That may be true in other countries but not in the United States, we would just raise the debt limit and print more money.

Resisting Paying Taxes

Is there a way to resist paying taxes and get away with it? Tax free contributions to charitable donations might be one way to avoid taxes. Maybe we need a form for conscientious war objectors to designate where their tax money will be spent. But, when I tell United Fund solicitors that "I have given a large donation to the Salvation Army," they said "give us the money and we will direct it to the Salvation Army." Then I say, "yes, but if I give my money directly to the Salvation Army they will not only get my donation but some of your money" and that is the group I would like to see prosper. That was an actual conversation.

An article that appeared in *The Week* magazine in July 2011 reported a man earning eleven million dollars a year and paying no income tax. The man was not identified. I wish *The Week* had published some information on how he did it. What kind of person is this? Does this person have any respect for our institutions? What was the source of his income? And, why are our legislators letting him get away with it?

The United States has a lot of hidden taxes and one might argue against paying them. It is a good idea to examine all utility bills since that is often a place where federal taxes are slipped in. When you pay your phone bill of $62.30 and note that $2.30 is for federal taxes you can withhold that amount with a note saying you object to the feds getting the phone company to collect taxes for them since you object to the way the feds spend the money. Of course, you might have your phone service disconnected.

As a stamp collector I have many stamps in my collection that have had a war tax attached to them, announced and unannounced. Many Canada stamps during World War I had "War Tax 2 cents" overprinted on the regular stamp. Other countries had the price on the stamp listed as 6 + 3 with the 3 designated for the military or some other activity presently short of funds.

The best statement one could make was simply refusing to pay a tax by ignoring the tax bill when it arrives. If you wish to be dramatic then you can declare that you refuse to pay. When the feds come to get you then you can make a public statement, if the media will cooperate. Once, in a protest, one of our protesters got his head rapped with no media coverage to publicize the event and so there was no reward for the suffering.

If you object to the war and military budget you can figure out the percentage of the budget that goes to the military and deduct that amount from the tax you pay. Again, that would be a statement of protest, but you will be breaking the law and probably suffer some consequence as the result of it.

Some taxpayers include a protest statement with their taxes. One has to be careful in doing this since there is a law concerning "frivolous tax returns." Such a tax return would give you a day in court. One taxpayer wrote "don't spend it on five hundred dollar toilet seats." She was hauled into court for filing a frivolous return.

By the way, that five hundred dollar toilet seat that got so much publicity, was probably a screen for expenditures that were classified. When I was stationed on our side of the Iron Curtain in Germany I often found such things as common bolts, nuts and screws with high price tags. These were items that could have been purchased downtown for only a few cents. Indeed, military procurement contracts do need supervision. Case in point:the ridiculous expenditures on private security firms in Iraq.

Some protesters try to get in their protest by attempting to pay their taxes in coins. I am not certain this is legal in the United States since

I never considered this method of protesting but I do know coins are not legal tender is some countries over specified amounts.

There are hundreds of ads from lawyers on television concerning taxation. Many of them claim they will lower your tax bill by using their legal knowledge. This is probably true and if one has a large tax claim against them then it may be prudent to employ such a lawyer. It is a shame that in America the tax system is so unfair and complicated that we have to higher lawyers to explain it to us. This statement would also take in having to hire someone to fill out the 1040 for us.

One way that Fred beats the tax code is by working in the underground economy. He collects scrap metal and sells it to a dealer. One of his other activities was to buy a couple of goats and later peddle four goats. When he does repair and construction work for a neighbor he will give the neighbor a discount if he is paid in cash. These are illegal activities if he does not pay taxes on his income from those activities.

If the taxes really bother you it might be best to change your life style. To avoid paying the tax on gasoline you could start traveling by bicycle or walking to work. You can avoid the liquor tax by brewing and distilling your own stock, which by the way is another activity of Fred. You could take up a frugal lifestyle if taxes really bother you. These lifestyle changes are not really tax evasion and they are within the legal system. The goal is to avoid as much tax as possible or to minimize your tax payments where possible.

In the United States the courts have ruled that tax resisters have no right to avoid income taxes on religious grounds. Would we all join that religion if it declared otherwise? My objection in this sense is the tax break given to religious people by donations to religious enterprises even though their causes may be worthy. You know the amendment. I also object to religious enterprises getting tax breaks on property taxes. Many of these religious properties are on the most expensive and desirable lands of the community. Perhaps, okay, on the building of worship, but not okay on the rest of it like recreation halls, vehicles, and certain fund raisers.

The term **civil resistance** is often used to describe political action that relies on the use of non-violent methods by civil groups to challenge a particular power, force, policy or regime. An effective form of counter resistance, as politicians well know, is to undermine the credibility of the target. How can we trust the government to handle this problem when we saw what happened in Louisiana? Look at Medicare and then you will wonder why we can't trust the government to run a universal health care system. Newt used this method very effectively in his brief but illustrious government career.

Other methods, used for coercion, other than demonstrations, include strikes, slow downs, boycotts and sit ins. In many foreign countries emigration is an excellent action. The thousands of young Americans who went to Canada for refuge during the Viet Nam War had an impact on the final decisions made during that war. However, most countries would be glad to get people moving out of their domains rather than regret it, especially if there are laws to prevent them taking their money with them.

More peaceful resistance would be such things as candle light vigils, parades, and internet bombardment. You and I have been besieged with petitions to send in to our members of Congress. Most of these are pre-printed and all you have to do to save the whales is to sign it and send it in. I wonder if any member of Congress pays attention to these. What bugs me is that when I get a petition where the cause is worthwhile it also comes with a request for contributions. How many petitions, how many signatures, would it take to get a member of Congress to react to it. If you write a letter to them concerning a particular topic you will usually get a response with some kind of blather about it. You won't get a response if you sign a pre-printed petition devised by some organization since most members of Congress realize that the purpose is to get contributions and not necessarily to change legislation.

It is hoped that civil disobedience is related to a special cause and not related to the ego of the resister or the resisting group. We also hope that the resistance is for the improvement of society or the improvement of the law making mechanism of that society. The resister has an obligation to champion a worthy cause and the government has an obligation to listen to the resistor and give attention to that cause. **The government should look upon a resister as a person trying to improve the government rather than someone who is the enemy of that government.** However, there are some resisters who are outright anarchists and madmen who use tactics of terror and intimidation to gain their ends. These also should not be ignored.

A Puzzled Look at Our Tax System

Should we revolt and protest over our complicated tax system. Hell yes. But, who in this country has the mental facility to separate the entanglement and come up with a fair and equitable system. The Internal Revenue Service takes a lot of the blame and is the most despised organization in the country. It's hard to understand that since the IRS doesn't make the laws, all they do is enforce them. My involvement with the IRS employees has always been positive, although not always working out to my benefit. So lay off the IRS and get on the backs of Congress.

Concerning taxes we seem to be operating in bizzaro land. Bush II and his partner Dick Cheney orchestrated tax cuts for the rich while declaring two wars. That couldn't possibly make sense to any rational person.

We still have the tax cuts in force. The rich were supposed to create jobs with the extra bonanza but they did not come through since their loyalty is to money rather than the country. I doubt that a person making twenty million dollars a year would suffer much if the income was reduced to nineteen million, or even eighteen million.

Perhaps a federal sales tax on all purchases except food is one answer. Some states, such as West Virginia, have a sales tax on food.

We have to realize that tax breaks is another form of spending. To many of our Congressmen eliminating a tax break is looked upon as the same as increasing taxes rather than a spending cut.

When Congress makes an adjustment in the tax code they often claim it is made in order for it to be more easily understood. A check of any modified tax law on the books will easily indicate that the language became more complicated and longer in length. This is not simplification.

The Flat Tax

It seems logical and simple that we should embrace the idea of a flat tax. Several national figures have added their names to the idea. Steve Forbes comes to mind. We should learn from others experiences.

Supporters of the flat tax, that is one uniform rate for income tax payers, regardless of wealth say it will eliminate tax cheating and bring in higher revenues than the graduated income tax.

The first group of countries that instituted a flat tax were the Baltic countries of Estonia, Latvia and Lithuania. All three of these countries are still n the same economic trouble as countries with different tax systems. You simply cannot spend more than you take in. All three of the countries have what could be termed generous welfare systems. Perhaps, these welfare payments were too generous and they should have been slashed to make ends meet. Of course, there are other areas of management where the budget could be decreased. In our country it seems to be that every legislator has some pet project that occupies his interests. Usually these projects are reflected in campaign contributions.

The problems of the three Baltics were numerous. Their exports to other countries of Europe were curtailed just after the tax "reform." They increased their borrowing. A 2011 report states that Estonia's foreign debt represents 131 percent of their GDP, Latvia's is 116 percent of GDP and Lithuania's is 72 percent.

Riots broke out in Latvia in 2009 when protesters marched against the declining economy. The government was forced to resign and a new government was installed. Too bad we can't do that.

When the rioting was starting to spread to the rest of Europe the International Monetary Fund and the European Union gave Latvia a $10.5 million dollar loan with the requirement they hold their budget deficit to less than five percent. Latvia could not meet the five percent mandate.

The Latvian riots spread to Lithuania. An estimated crowd of seven thousand demonstrators threw eggs and stones at windows of government buildings to protest economic austerity measures. You can't have it both ways. Our government seems to think you can.

One fact seems to be ignored by our legislators and that is corporate profits and CEO wages are at an all time high while the wages of the average worker are continually decreasing. Trying to find the percentage of our work force working at minimum wage is a daunting task.

The Lithuanian parliament has ordered pay cuts on all public sector workers and lowered the value of state pensions. The Prime Minister ordered four thousand government service jobs to be eliminated.

We must acknowledge that cutting the government work force throws these employees into the unemployed ranks competing for jobs in an ever decreasing job market.

Estonian lawmakers say they would like to keep the budget deficit below three percent in order to qualify for membership in the euro common currency.

These moves by the Baltic governments have implications for our own problems. When statistics concerning unemployment of the three Baltics come forth they seldom include the migration of their citizens to the rest of Europe. Without this migration the unemployment rate of these countries would probably around fifteen percent.

No one can be certain that the Baltics would have been better off with a graduated income tax. The point is that the flat tax did not solve their budget woes. The flat tax merely reduces the tax burden of the rich while increasing it on the middle class and it will require large amounts of social spending to reduce the budget woes.

As to the flat tax, it is an unfair idea that the billionaire pays the same tax rate as the worker in a fast food restaurant. One of our flat tax opponents stated that a twenty percent flat tax would barely be seen by a person with a million dollar income whereas a flat tax of twenty percent would be a disaster to a person with a fifteen thousand dollar minimum wage income.

It is only fair that a tax should be of such a nature that it reflects the ability of those taxed to pay on a sliding scale according to their income.

VII PROTESTS AND ORGANIZATION

Organizing a Protest and a Protest Group

If you are organizing a group for some particular cause there are several techniques for achieving solidarity. These may be in the form of dues and membership cards. Soliciting funds other than from membership dues is another technique which is successful if the cause is inflammatory. . Most people do not like that proposition if they cannot see the necessity of the funds. It would be difficult to solicit funds to try to change the deduction allowance on income tax.

In any war or conflict it is better to have a failed offense than a failed defense. To be successful one cannot sit back and wait, the fight must move forward.

In organizing a group it would be advantageous to have adopted a protest song such as "We Shall Overcome." There are many such songs and chants that have been effective. In the Vietnam War there were, "Hell no, we won't go" and "LBJ how many kids did you kill today."

It would also be advantageous to have a banner. If the color red can be put in the banner so much the better since that color has proved to have more psychological advantages to mental alertness than any other color.

How about a slogan from Star Wars? "May the Force Be With You."

The Nazi Party of Germany had a very successful symbolic organization to instill loyalty in its members and make their organization appealing to the masses. We won't comment on their leadership decisions. They had two inspiration pieces of music, one specializing in song and the other in marching. They had a dramatic flag and armbands and they had a binding phrase, "Heil Hitler." The loyalty of their adherents was beyond belief.

Hitler and his henchmen, among them Goring and Goebbels, marched on the headquarters of their rivals in the SA, killed their leaders outright and locked many of the followers in prisons where they were convinced to join the Nazis or face death. The day after the onslaught Goebbels told the press that they had avoided a takeover of the government by the rabble SA. The public bought the explanation. The leader Hindenburg even sent Hitler a congratulatory telegram praising him for his quick and effective action. It didn't dawn on the German people that Hitler had actually killed off the opposition and taken over the power of the state.

There are many ways to organize a peaceful protest, but there are some common aspects of all protest planning. First of all you have to determine if you are going to be loud, moderate or silent. The decision should be evident based on the nature of the proposed protest. If the protest concerns the execution of someone then a silent protest would seem to be in order. If the protest concerns some government failure then it should be loud and clear.

A second consideration would be to educate the public in advance about the nature of the protest. This can be done through news releases to the media or at some gathering such as the meeting of the township supervisors where an announcement could be made. Most often, the news media will ignore your announcement unless you can add some spice to it.

The location for the protest should be in a highly visible area such as a community park, courthouse street, or the area of concern of the protest. You would want a protest about beach access or public beach fees down at the beach rather than in the central park.

If possible get a high profile speaker to join your cause and see that he or she has amplifying devices to aid the speech or rallying cries.

Leaders of the protest should themselves be available to speak and discuss their problem with the media. However, the leaders should make every effort to see that they are all on the same page.

One of the first rules of organizing a protest is to check the local laws concerning such activities. Do you need a permit? What could cause a permit to be legally denied? Can you set up road or street blocks and redirect traffic? What safety measures are expected to be installed?

One main concern is how will you handle disruptive behavior or destruction of property by participants in your group. If a peaceful protest is really your intent then make a deal to have police nearby that you can turn to for assistance. In one protest we had instructed the crowd before our march. When one of the marchers threw a cabbage into a plate glass window we immediately pointed him out to the police and had him arrested.

Another situation that comes to mind was when I was in basic training in Arkansas and the temperature was over ninety degrees Fahrenheit. We had been sweating at exercises for about an hour. The master sergeant in charge said he was not satisfied with our enthusiasm and would keep us for an extra half hour which cut into our lunch time. One of the recruits blurted out "Shit." The sergeant wanted to know who the culprit was or we would get another half hour tacked on. No one came forward to identify the culprit as we stood at attention. The culprit was about to step forward when his buddy restrained him. After about ten minutes soldiers started dropping to the ground. I don't know if this was faked or not but I felt like dropping to the ground also. After about a dozen men were laying on the ground we were dismissed. A captain who was watching the situation came over to one of the men lying on the ground and asked him if he wanted to go to the base hospital. The man, obviously dazed, said, "No sir, I want to stay with the troops." The captain ordered a deuce and a half truck driver to take all the fallen men to the base hospital for a check-up.

One of the best methods for handling potential disruptions is to appoint group leaders and have the group divided under their command. If the group is going to be particularly large then the group leaders can wear armbands designating them as such and they can work around the crowd and also be a source of information to members of the crowd. The armbands should be numbered and to whom it was issued and not be easily duplicated.

There are a lot of complicated requirements to protesting in Washington DC and there should be. Some internet sources detail the steps one must take in order to do this.

What Kind of Protest?

When deciding how to protest a legitimate grievance, special thought must be given to the type of strategy that would best fit the situation. If one is protesting the price of bread or gasoline it would seem inappropriate to set fire to a government building. The appropriate response would be to protest by boycotting those products if it was at all feasible. A person may perceive a logical form of disobedience, but engage in another form that does not match the complaint. For instance, stopping traffic to protest gasoline prices, with the idea somehow it will lower gasoline prices. It inconveniences people that are really not part of the protest and may jeopardize their employment.

The price of gasoline should be a free market enterprise and the actual price determined by fair competition among the producers. The word here is "free." If there is collusion then that is another facet of the problem. When collusion occurs then we do not have a free market enterprise and government action is necessary to correct the situation. If our government doesn't believe in free enterprise they should have the decency to admit it.

When there is a departure from justice then civil disobedience may be necessary to correct that injustice, or at least, to let the authorities know that their injustice has not gone unobserved. When Oliver North was asked to speak in Erie, Pennsylvania he was sponsored by a local bank and paid twenty five thousand dollars for a one hour appearance. It was my feeling that he should have been in prison rather than freely walking around. The laws he broke were out-and-out treason. What was particularly disturbing he became the darling of the law-and-order crowd, and still is for that matter. I contacted the bank and voiced my complaint and when their response was unsatisfactory I withdrew my money and cashed in all Certificates of Deposit with them. Later, when I talked to an employee of the bank, I was informed that about fifty people did likewise. The bank later issued a public statement that they were not responsible for the invitation, it was a committee appointed to invite speakers to the city and they had financed that committee.

I can understand the motivation of Oliver North for breaking the law. What I do hold against him was his refusal to take the consequences of his action. He could have defended his actions as necessary in the light of the political situation and perhaps appeared as a noble figure. What was also disturbing is the fact that President Reagan was not under investigation for the multiple disregard of the law. There was a weak attempt to investigate Reagan's role, in this, near the end of his term.

A problem in our society is "whom to blame" when things go wrong. In the case just discussed should I have gone to the committee, if there was such an organization.? Congress avoids this problem of responsibility by appointing committees to look into everything from soup-to-nuts. When the final vote is tallied and some unacceptable result is brought forth they can pass the blame on to someone other than themselves. For instance, they have no guts for a pay raise vote but tied it in their frequent salary increases to the rise in inflation. I don't believe there is a feature in place for the decrease in inflation. Is there such a thing as a negative inflation? (oxymoron)

The Case of Oliver North

Since my initial reaction, stated above, to Oliver North breaking federal law, I have come to look at his actions from a different perspective. When the chips-were-down he certainly would have been a revolutionary leader. Here is his story as best as I can tell it in a shortened form. Judge him for yourself.

North came into the public spotlight as a result of his participation in the Iran-Contra Affair, a political scandal of the late 1980s, in which he claimed partial responsibility for the sale of weapons via intermediaries to Iran, with the profits being channeled to the rebel Contras in Nicaragua. He was reportedly responsible for the establishment of a covert network, which aided the Contras. Several laws prohibited the appropriation of U.S. Funds by intelligence agencies for that purpose at that time, so those who wanted to support the Contras had to come up with some other method of funding. North allegedly, maybe he admitted it, funneled money from his organization, "National Endowment for the Preservation of Liberty" through various banks and eventually to the Contras.

Weapons and airplane parts were sold to Iran which was also against prevailing laws. In November 1986, the sale of these weapons was made public. North was dismissed by President Reagan and in July 1987 he was summoned to testify before televised hearings of a joint Congressional committee that was formed to investigate Iran-Contra and its actions concerning the law.

In all of this, it was brought out that Manuel Noriega was paid one million dollars in cash from the sale of U.S. Arms to Iran, for the Panamanian leader's help in destroying Nicaraguan economic installations. Noriega was later arrested for drug trafficking and sentenced to a prison term. Some investigators tried to connect the money he received to this drug activity.

When North took the oath before his trial the photographic image became a national sensation and remains a historic archive photo today. It was an image that made him a public icon in many areas of the country, despite the fact that he broke the law and lied under that oath..

During the hearings, North admitted that he had lied to Congress, for which, among other things, he was later charged. He defended his actions by stating that he believed in the goal of aiding the Contras, whom he saw as freedom fighters and said that he viewed the Iran-Contra scheme as a "neat idea." He had also assisted in the shredding of documents related to the matter.

North was tried in 1988 in relation to his activities while at the National Security Council. He was indicted on sixteen felony counts, and, on May 4, 1989, he was initially convicted of three, which were: accepting an illegal gratuity; aiding and abetting in the obstruction of a congressional inquiry; and ordering the destruction of documents via his secretary. He was sentenced, by the U.S. District Judge on July 5, 1989, to a three-year suspended prison term, two years' probation, $150,000 in fines, and 1,200 hours community service.

Not so fast Justice, slow down. On July 20, 1990, with the help of the American Civil Liberties Union North's convictions were vacated, after the appeals court found that witnesses in his trial might have been affected by his immunized congressional testimony. Because North had been granted limited immunity for his Congressional testimony, the law prohibited the independent counsel from using that testimony as part of a criminal case against him.

While the defense could show no specific instance in which North's congressional testimony was used in his trial, the Court of Appeals ruled that the trial judge had made an insufficient examination of the issue. Consequently, North's convictions were reversed. It never went to a higher court.

I have said somewhere else that "Lawyers are scum until you need one." So it is with the ACLU which is constantly maligned by right wing zealots. The ACLU is scum until you need it to defend your own civil rights.

Protesting people may be able to justify their actions based on the following (1) forcing the people with the dominant opinion to defend their views (2) illustrating a departure from justice (3) encourage a democratic exchange of ideas (4) getting a change in legislation or civil behavior, and (5) exposing their viewpoint to public scrutiny.

The disobedient action that is taken should be tailored to the (1) social environment of the time (2) the political situation (3) the actions taken by other groups or individuals concerning this subject, (4) the target of the protest, and (5) the expected outcome of the protest.

Certainly, we must believe that questioning the prevailing views of the time is one of the highest virtues of a person in society. We have an obligation to go beyond the obligation to follow the law if an injustice is perpetrated. If those statements are true, and I do not doubt the truth of them, then we have an obligation to dissent when we find, or feel, our laws are unjust. We have an obligation to replace an ineffective government bogged down in bickering or a government beholding to a privileged class, at least in our form of democracy.

It is the government's responsibility to insure a "level playing field." Exorbitant profits are always the result of collusion or a monopoly in free enterprises after the initial burst of innovation has subsided and the profits of this innovation are realized. The profits from the extraction of natural resources should be treated differently than the profits from patents and inventions. The former belong to all of us while the latter belongs to the inventor.

Motives

It is possible that a person (actor) might engage in civil disobedience without examining the motive behind the action, or more importantly, the consequences of that action. Does the actor consider the merit behind the cause under consideration and thus form a defense for the act. It is assumed the act of protest would be legal and if the act is illegal what could be the consequences of the act to the actor. Is the act being performed because there are no other options in seeking the change requested? Is the cause so important to the actor that incarceration or physical harm are not reason to abort the project or protest?

In a just society people have a moral and political obligation to follow the law. We assume we can make changes in the system by following some sort of natural philosophy, such as "all men are created equal." That philosophy of course is limited and although sweeping in extent is never-the-less is false, not true, a lie, but it can be a starting point for dialogue and its truth or falseness can be pointed out in the dialogue.

When Jews in Ferdinand and Isabella's Spain were given the choice of converting to Catholicism or sacrifice their lives, many of them chose the latter. So it is a question of philosophy that what sacrifice is one willing to make to advance the cause? It is easy to have moral consistency if one's life is not in danger. Unless there is an afterlife then death is final as far as the individual is concerned. In order to be philosophically correct then a person would have to willingly go to prison for breaking the law in order to further the cause or create doubt in the mind of authority concerning their position on the matter that you have introduced by civil disobedience. Although the Amish in America disagree with much of the law, they obey the law because they have consented to its rule over them as well as other groups of citizens. **Conforming to a law does not mean that you are agreeing with its moral status.**

People have an obligation to follow the law if it is just. Some laws are patently unjust and there is no moral obligation to follow it, but there might be such intimidation that it would be unwise to object to it, especially in a society where police power is unchecked. Disobeying the law should be the last resort, but if the law is patently unjust then only by protest, peaceful or otherwise, can one hope to change the law. When asked why he was in jail, Thoreau replied something like "why are you not in here with me?"

Can we use the same grueling legal methods forever in a quest for justice? Those in power would of course oppose the change or they would have already made that change. It appears that legal channels to oppose change are not really effective. **Power is not easily relinquished by those who have it**. So, in facing the stone wall of authority, civil disobedience is the last resort.

If all legal avenues have proved useless then if the cause is dear to one's heart then illegal action is necessary. The history of John Brown and his objections to slavery are an excellent example of such a situation. History has painted John Brown as a "wide eyed radical" rather than a person of moral character whose cause was just. John Brown tried to use legal channels but of course did not get anywhere since slavery was condoned by much legislation. The violent methods used by John Brown and his followers were not acceptable in a legal society and he was legally executed. In this instance it would not be appropriate to say "not acceptable in a civilized society." John Brown was confident that his form of civil disobedience was the last resort. "You have to shake them in order to wake them up"

Sometimes a person is incarcerated under a law that is prevalent at the time of incarceration and when the law has changed still remains incarcerated. Such, I believe, is the case in many instances of illegal drug abuse. One can justify the continued incarceration under the assumption that at the time of the incarceration, the law or laws have been violated.

Advice

It is in the best interests of a revolutionary group to coordinate their efforts with other like-minded groups concerning the same subject. (How did you react to the term "revolutionary or didn't you react at all?" We assume the cause is one of a minority group since a majority group could conceivably overturn the legislation. Blacks and Hispanics seemed to have been on the same page in the Watts Riots since more than half of the people arrested were Hispanic.

In seeking the cooperation and enforcement of other minority groups it is best to get an agreement before the action begins. Perhaps the situation in the Watts Area of Los Angeles was such that the minority groups did not need coordination since they were all living under the same conditions.

If your group believes the cause is just then coordination with other groups is unnecessary. But, look at the parable circulated after World War II. " When the Nazis rounded up the Jews I didn't care since I was not a Jew. When the Nazis rounded up the gypsies, it didn't matter since I was not a gypsy. When they arrested etc. Then when they came for my group, there was no one around to help us." So, it might be wise to consider the old adage, "there is strength in numbers", before you start your revolution.

If you solicit the support of other groups and they do not offer their support then that does not mean your position should not be defended. They might not want to cooperate for many reasons, fear being one of them. Another reason for not rocking the boat is that they are doing reasonably well or marginally well under the current system and the current laws. Your group might be competition to them and they would welcome your demise. In the colonial days of America the Natives were so in competition among themselves that they failed to see the intruders as the enemy. Had there been cooperation among the different tribes instead of hostility they may have been able to delay the takeover for many centuries.

Protesting can be justified if there is a high probability that some changes will be enacted as a result of the protesting. This assumption includes exposing society to harm such as creating a division in society. If the poor attack the rich, then the rich will have to band together to protect their interests. For some reason what hasn't been identified to my satisfaction was the division of our political society into two confrontational camps with little room in the middle ground.

One of the problems with democracy, such as ours, is that it tends to give dissidents the idea that they can only affect changes by decisive actions. There is a tendency to go on such things as spur of the moment wildcat strikes, sit-ins and down-town congregating. Spur of the moment actions are not coordinated, have no leaders and no particular agenda is presented that can be corrected by government action on the spur of the moment. These meetings foster disrespect for the law long after they have disbanded. **Disrespect for the law is not good in a democracy.**

If one protesting group has success in affecting changes then it may encourage other groups to do the same and engage in protesting to achieve their ends. As a student in graduate schools I was always appalled when another student shouted out his opinion rather than raise his hand and wait his turn to speak. What struck me most was that the student shouting out had his opinion expressed immediately while I, who raised my hand, had to wait until four or five others had expressed their opinions. It is like that with spontaneous protesting. The cause, if identifiable, is immediately given attention while a planned protest must wait its turn.

Some protesting can be used to delay an action believed to be detrimental to society. An example of this would be the building of a dam which would destroy the habitat along the course of the stream being impounded. Protesters might show up and chain themselves over the roadway leading to the site. They might damage vehicles used in construction. It would be unwise for them to threaten the workers or the managers of that construction. This type of protest must be sustained for any positive results. Once the protest subsides the project will continue. At least the protesters might fill justified in giving the wildlife living along the stream banks a few more weeks of living in their homesteads.

Philosophy: If the harm being inflicted by the law is of unacceptable proportion then this harm being inflicted by the protest is justifiable. Sometimes the harm seems so overwhelming that the protester has no personal choice but to take severe action. This is often the case in the assassination of government leaders who have been tyrants and architects of divisive legislation. Unfortunately, there are people with a mindset to assassinate leaders for no reason other than they are leaders. However, some violence might be necessary to preserve the rights and civil liberties that have been suspended.

Successful protest or civil disobedience should have, as its target and made obvious, a distinct law or action that the protesters find objectionable. There should be no ambiguity over what is being protested. If the protest would manage to get the law changed, what is the harm to people who have been enjoying the benefits of that law? Perhaps we shouldn't care about them.

The mainstream media usually selects a position on certain issues and are unlikely to give much attention to issues that they do not support. In this case civil disobedience can get their attention and force them to publicize the view of protest. Once the media has responded, the protest can be used to give views that will inform and educate the public. Continued protest of a subject might give such a higher cost of combating the protests that the authorities will yield to the protesters, especially if no harm will come to those who do not benefit from the aims of the protesters.

The protester (or a reporter) can ask these questions of the action. Does my method of protest meet the requirements of a legal protest and is my protest for the right reason? Is my reason for protest based on fact, or is it simply emotion? For instance, one may protest the assumed fact that no rich person has ever been executed for the crime of murder. Therefore, since the sentence might not be unjust, the carrying out of the sentence is not fair, I am justified in protesting the legality of capital punishment. So, when the facts are in, the reason for the protest might not be justified. Even if the reason for the protest was justified, why did the protester choose a particular method of protest, like silent candlelight protest or dynamiting the execution building, thus slowing down executions.

Too often legislators, or others, take up a cause that really has no interest to them. They merely want to be re-elected. Therefore they join protesters at the march or rally in order to secure votes of the black majority or the followers of white supremacy. Their speeches are tailored to the audience in front of them. It is both tragic and humorous that many legislators have engaged in bashing gays and lesbians when they themselves were homosexual. Many supported and protested homosexuality without scientific knowledge of the subject. Senator Trent Lott said that homosexuality was a "disease." What crowd was he playing to? Homosexual protests is a good example of perseverance. Those early demonstrators who got their heads bashed in should be martyrs to those who have benefited from their actions. Actually, we are all indebted to them for erasing much of the legislation that was unfair to a segment of society.

However, there is another way to look at the gay rights protests. Some advocates who had joined the protests were doing it merely to get votes in a particular district or meeting. We admire those who advocate the rights of others but we must not go overboard when their motivation was not for the correct reasons.

Bolshevik Tactic

The successful Hitler coup claiming that he had saved the country from the SA was preceded by the Bolsheviks in 1917 when they orchestrated serious doubts in people's minds about the Interim Government's intentions to hold a general election. This delay in holding elections permitted the Bolsheviks to claim the temporary government had fallen into the hands of the pro-tsarist regime, the counter revolutionaries and they, the Bolsheviks, used this excuse to justify their own seizure of power.

When the Tsar had been deposed a Council of Ministers had already been in place to lead the country. One of the ministers Nabokov, who headed the secretariat of that coalition, wrote, "the endless agonizing sessions of the Council of Ministers in which distension and the smoldering of obvious hostility of some individuals toward others prevented any progress."

In our congress the same situation can be said to exist. Let me repeat: "the endless agonizing sessions of the Council of Ministers (in this case Congress) in which dissension and the smoldering of obvious hostility of some individuals toward others prevented any progress."

In old Russia a rich estate might contain several small scattered villages. The peasants worked the land around their own village. After emancipation of the serfs (peasants) they continued to work the land, but as renters and share croppers.

When the upheaval began many manor houses of the estates were torched by the peasants. Fearing for their lives the gentry usually gave their peasants the plots they had worked. Shortly after the time of emancipation the peasants formed village communes and selected their leaders. These leaders would keep order in the village, control crime and bargain for the produced crops.

So once the revolution took hold in the cities the peasants already had a system of management that tended to defend their interests against outsiders, such as state officials, merchants,town people, as well as peasants from neighboring villages. The leaders of the communes then assumed control of the estate after the revolution. These small villages did not suffer the upheaval that occurred in the cities after the revolution. There was little conflict between rich and poor peasants since they all had a voice in their government. This changed when the Bolsheviks took over and began class warfare on a grand scale.

The peasants of 1917 were timid in confiscating the lands of the gentry at that time. Their fathers had tried it in 1905 during the revolution that followed the disastrous War with Japan and a weakened aristocracy. In the 1905 revolution many of the peasants had begun to work on parcels of aristocratic holdings with the idea of entitlement. Once the Tsar's government regained control their agents went out into the countryside, held trials, and executed thousands of peasants who had commandeered the aristocratic lands.

Usually a revolution is instigated because of the political bankruptcy of the leaders. All social revolutions are by their very nature violent. When mass revolt occurs it is necessary to defend civilization against the instincts of the crowd. In a revolt where hostages are taken, especially if the hostages are from the authority, mob trials eventually become lynch mobs based mostly on hearsay evidence or simply on the power of the mob in charge. Anyone caught up in a lynch mob mentality would do well to remember and be able to identify the lynchers. All efforts must be made to bring hostages, taken by the mob, to a legal trial.

Decline in Union Membership

The decline in union membership is a threat to democratic stability. Why shouldn't there be a decline in industrial union membership since there was a tremendous decline in industrial workers in the country as jobs were shipped overseas.

It was the unions that brought the income of workers to a living wage. It was the unions that gave American workers pride.

Unions are the battalions limiting the abuses of management. Teachers unions at the college and university levels have abandoned their responsibility in checking the abuse to adjunct faculty whose part-time wages are about one third of a full time member for the same amount of work. Of course, looking from the standpoint of management and the bottom line, why pay one professor full time benefits and high wages when you can hire three part-time professors for one third of the cost.

Back in the late 1950's I was the president of our high school teachers association. At that time cheap Japanese goods were flooding the country and people were enjoying these inexpensive products of high quality. I pointed out that these were threats to our own industries which produced the same products. There was much discussion of this topic at one meeting and most agreed that they liked the cheap Japanese televisions and recording devices. I remember that meeting with clarity and was reminded later by others in the meeting, that I said "Wait until they start sending over cheap Japanese teachers."

Thus in the ensuing years our television industry and high tech electronic sound equipment was replaced by foreign manufacturing. We don't make clothing or shoes anymore. No need to expand this to the other products.

A note of final irony. When I retired from college teaching at age 75 there were fifteen members in my department, three of them were immigrants from foreign countries.

All revolutions by their nature are illegal. In any revolution **the only real power is power**. So who has the power in America, the rich and their corporations. The Supreme Court has ruled that the corporations have the same political status as an individual and can contribute to political campaigns with the status of an individual.

The only way to combat the power of the rich and their corporations is to strengthen the unions and associations which represent the middle class.

One could argue that the destruction of union power began back in 1981 when President Reagan fired the air traffic controllers and invited the union busters to go to work. No other groups sprung to the defense of the air traffic controllers and so they were plowed under as a union.

The Yugoslav Ploy

One of the problems with protesting is that the **authorities usually look upon a protester as an enemy rather than as someone trying to improve society.** Authorities look out at the crowd and fear the numbers and fear going out among them. The usual response to protest is for the authorities to invite the protesters to sit down and "let's talk things over." This may seem logical but in these confrontations the authorities are not in a position to be intimidated, which might be a key factor in effecting social change. .

I was part of a college group organized in 1973 to study the education and social systems in Yugoslavia that were under communist control at that time. The caper was paid for by reducing the debt Yugoslavia owed to the United States after the big war.

Basically there were three different enterprise options available in Yugoslavia to the citizens at that time. These were (1) outright government ownership (2) individual ownership, and (3) cooperatives.

University students had quit classes and staged protests for free higher education at the government schools, better division of government run enterprise profits and reorganization of student cooperatives.

The walk-out and demonstrations were in full swing when legendary Marshall Tito was forced to go on national television to address the problem. We were in a small library room with about twenty students watching the television.

Marshall Tito started out his speech by saying, "I will not go against the students."

A cheer went up from about half the viewers. A few of the young women near me burst into tears as they hugged each other.

Then after about ten minutes of blather Tito went on to say, "I ask the students to go back to your classrooms and arrange meetings with the administrators and discuss your problems and thereby find solutions."

When the speech was over there was jubilation, but it was not unanimous. A young woman who was one of the organizers actually got up on a table and called for attention which she received. She began, "You dummies, you lost and don't realize it. You'll go back to your classes and nothing will have been gained. We will be divided and conquered."

Several of the students said they were happy and "amen" to Tito's suggestion, or was it a mandate. We observers did not have the communist mentality to know which.

Four of us invited the woman on the table to have dinner with us to get her views on the situation as well as the Yugoslav brand of communism.

Her name was Sophie or Sophia and she spoke very good English. She said the protests were not about education but about the division of profits from enterprises such as the restaurant in which we were dining, which was a government operation with an A rating. She said that no private or cooperative restaurant could receive an A rating since the government wanted an unfair advantage over the competition when the tourists came.

At the end of the fiscal year and sometimes in the middle of the fiscal year the employees came together to vote on how to share the profits of the enterprise. There were two ways to distribute the profits. One was to divide the profits equally among all the workers. The other distribution method was to divide the profits according to percentage of wages. The higher paid managers would get more of the profits.

Sofie said when the division of profits were put to a vote the manager would start off by saying, "I vote for percentage." Since it was not a secret ballot all workers who feared for their jobs would go along with the managers.

The students, many of whom were employed, wanted a secret ballot or a legal acknowledgment that the profits would be equally divided. After all, it was a communist enterprise where everyone was supposed to be equal.

Riot vs Protest

A major problem exists when a protest becomes an undisciplined protest. The situation turns into a carnival atmosphere and the purpose of the protest is shunted aside. The events become absurd rather than heroic. Some documented evidence exists that a demonstration in Athens was infiltrated by police who deliberately turned a peaceful protest into a riot situation, thus giving the government authority to step in. Unfortunately, two of the planted infiltrators were killed during the melee and their identities exposed.

If the demonstration crowd is large and people are not able to be identified then the criminal element, which seems to be in every crowd, breaks loose and engages in looting and destruction of property. An order of shoot-to-kill looters would stop this action almost immediately, but we are in a civilized country and we believe stealing a television set is not worth a person's life. In Columbia and Venezuela, more often than not, looters are shot rather than apprehended. Newspaper editorials do not object and refer to the looters as "anti-socials."

Leaders of a protest have an obligation to insure discipline and as soon as one member beaks this requirement that member should be removed in some manner. A mob mentality is not desirable when conducting a serious demonstration.

The Watts Riot of 1965

The events known as the Watts Riots began on August 11, 1965 when a black man, Marquette Frye was stopped by a white highway patrolman Lee Minikus. The stop was made for suspicion of driving under the influence of alcohol.

A crowd began to gather at the scene of the arrest and a heated exchange of words were passed between the crowd and other officers who had arrived on the scene. The exchange became heated and it touched off a run of violence centered in the commercial district of the Watts area of Los Angeles.

The riot lasted six days and resulted in more than forty million dollars worth of property damage. For six days the rioters burned automobiles, looted and damaged commercial enterprises such as liquor and grocery stores. Policeman were afraid to enter Watts for fear of their lives. Several white male drivers who were trying to pass through the section were yanked from their cars and beaten.

The governor ordered 14,000 California National Guard troops to the scene and a curfew zone was established. When it was all under control thirty four people were dead and about one thousand were injured enough to require medical attention. About four thousand arrests were made.

Throughout the riot, many people said the blame for the riot was not local people protesting the living conditions of the Watt's area, but the work of outside agitators. This is a ploy used over the centuries,

"Our people are not rioters, it is the work of others." In most European riots of the late nineteenth century, more often than not, the civil unrest was blamed on Germans if it was not in Germany and Jews no matter where the riots occurred. This, of course, gave governments an excuse to harass the Jews, even though the allegations were completely without merit.

So it was also said with the first Watts Riot. Outside agitators had come in to encourage the crowd No one seemed to know when these agitators had arrived or who they were.

An official investigation, under the direction of Governor Pat Brown, unearthed a plethora of legitimate grievances and discontent among the residents of that area. Unemployment was around seventeen percent, most housing was declared substandard, and the schools were deemed inadequate.

The report was filed. So what? City and state officials failed to implement measures to improve the conditions in Watts found by the governor's commission. It was no surprise to sociologists when Watts erupted again a few years later.

VIII POPULATION CONSIDERATIONS

In 1930 there were 2 billion people on earth. By 1960 the number had risen to 3 billion and by 1975 there were 4 billion. The next billion was added by 1987 and in 1995 we had 5.7 billion. In June 2011 the world population was just short of seven billion. Population experts predict that the world population will increase to 11 billion around the year 2050 and then level off.
The world population is increasing by 350,000 a day, more than a million people are added every three days. If we are to give each of the new babies one glass of milk and a half loaf of bread each day, then it will take more than 25,000 new cows and 500 new acres planted in wheat. The world is decreasing in those commodities rather than increasing.

Most scientists predict that the increasing population will put a severe strain on earth resources. Wonder how they came to that conclusion? Poverty levels will rise and standards of living will decrease to miserable levels. However, other scientists believe we can feed this large population through technological advances and standards of living for most of the world will increase rather than decrease. They point to the fact that even though the population has quadrupled in the last century the world is no
worse off than it was a hundred years previously. In fact, life spans have increased dramatically for average people in that period of time.
Whether you believe that there are too many people or not, you will have to agree that people are a resource. Other people provide the things you need to live and be comfortable. In most instances, other people provide you with food, clothing and shelter. They provide you with transportation, medical care and recreation. People are a natural resource in every sense of the word.

In 1798 Thomas Malthus published a book in which he stated that the plant world multiplied by arithmetic proportion 2, 4, 6, 8, 10 and the human world by geometric proportion 2, 4, 8, 16, 32. If this continued, humans would outstrip their food supply and there would be warfare, famine and pestilence in dramatic numbers.

Since the time of Malthus there have been famines, wars and pestilence which killed millions of people. However, the population continued to rise as advances in medicine and producing food have kept more people alive. Most scientists agree that the advance in population numbers is mostly due to a decrease in death rates.

Some countries want an increase in population, especially those where old people outnumber young people. For instance, in the United States, the Social Security System which pays out huge sums of money to retired citizens as well as disabled and dependent citizens, needs a steady flow of money in order to keep operating. Unless drastic changes are made in the payout there will not be enough young working people compared to retirees in 20 years in the country to keep the system working.

Most countries would like Zero Population Growth (ZPG) which is the number of births required for a population to continue replacing itself without increase. Worldwide, the rate is 2.1 but in rich countries the number is 2.2 since many women in these countries choose not to have children.

Many young couples say they would only like to have two children, that is, to replace themselves. However, a couple is two and if they have two children, there are now four where before there were two. It's a no win situation.

The number 2.1 is the fertility replacement rate. The fertility rate is an estimate of the number of children a woman between the ages of 15 and 44 will have in her lifetime. These rates are calculated on present births per thousand and female populations in a given country.

In 2011, the following fertility rates were calculated: Niger 7.6, Uganda 6.7, Mali 6.4, Pakistan 3.2, Venezuela 2.4, Mexico 2.3, U.S. 2.06, U.K. 1.9, Australia 1.7, Canada 1.58, China 1.54, Germany 1.4, and Japan 1.2. Generally the fertility rates are the lowest in Europe and the highest in Africa.

The fertility rates have shown some changes in the last fifteen years. For instance, it was 5.6 in Mexico in 1995, 3.9 in India and 1.6 in Japan. The situation in Japan can be described as panic since their young women are not having children. Their immigration laws practically eliminate any newcomers to the country and they have to rely on their own people production to maintain social programs. They have one of the most homogeneous racial make-ups in the world.

Population studies are usually based on the crude birth rate (CBR) which is the number of births in a year based on a population of 1000. The crude death rate is the number of deaths in a year based on a population of 1000. The U.S. CBR is 15 and the CBD is 9. Since the U.S. Population is 312,000,000 we multiply this with the difference in CBR-CBD, six times 312,000 (not 312,000,000) and find the U.S. Population increasing by 1,872,,000 each year, at the present rate.

If we take the yearly increase per 1,000 (6) and divide it by 10 we get the percent of increase. If we divide that (.6) into 70 we get the years it would take to double our population (117). We should divide into 72 but 70 is easier to work with and gives us a good approximation. This number is based on the amount of growth at 1

% a year. If you put a dollar into a bank account at one percent a year it would take 72 years before you had two dollars in that account.

One consideration of the crude birth rate based on a population of 1000 is that in many instances half of that population would be male and half of the rest would be females who are not of reproductive age. However, the system gives us some idea of population dynamics and is accurate enough for strategic planning purpose.

The increase in birth rate is not the only factor affecting the United States population, there is immigration and emigration, the number of people coming into the country and the number of people leaving the country. One very comprehensive study of illegal Mexicans coming into the U.S. was made in 1994. The conclusion was that Mexicans were illegally coming into the country at the rate of slightly more than one thousand a day. Studies indicate that this hasn't changed much in the last ten years. When this factor and other considerations is extrapolated the doubling of the U.S. Population is expected around the year 2055. Ironically, that is the year in which the Social Security fund is expected to disappear. The fund is supposedly solvent until 2040.

If the food supply remains static and the population doubles it does not take much mathematics to calculate that there is only half the amount of food available per person. That also means there is only half the amount of resources available per person.

If there are twenty of us sitting in a room and we each have a lunch of a cheeseburger and a milkshake and all of a sudden twenty people come into the room and we are forced to share our lunch, so we end up with half a cheeseburger and half a milkshake. Get it. How do we deal with it? Perhaps we should be satisfied with half of what we have today.

Throughout history increases in population have been managed in three ways which are (1) decreasing the number of people (2) increasing the food supply, and (3) limiting the number of births by birth control and family planning..

We have decreased the number of people within land areas through emigration, wars and genocide. In Rwanda, Africa in 1994, two different ethnic groups (Hutu and Tutsi) battled each other for four months for control of the land. When fighting ceased, over a million people had been slain. This reduced the Rwanda population by 12 percent.

The historic genocide of Nazi Germany and the Soviet Union need no elaboration here. The massive deaths of World War II had little impact on population. Despite all the deaths in wartime Japan their population was still larger after the war than before.

As you read this page, there are over fifty wars being fought somewhere in the world. The basic situation is a majority ethnic group trying to force a minority ethnic group to give up some of its land, its lives or resources. The resistance of the minority to do this leads to armed conflicts. When a minority group can break away from the majority it usually applies for admission as a country to the United Nations. If present trends continue the United Nations will double its membership in the next 50 years. Nations composing Chechens, Kurds and many other groups cannot be held in minority positions any longer. In 2011 South Sudan won its independence from Sudan.

Attempts to increase the food supply have met with success until recently. In 1995, world food production decreased from 1990. Grain, vegetable, meat, fruit and seafood production decreased by millions of tons in each category. World relief organizations simply could not deliver enough food to the starving people of the world. Food production in 2010 was static compared to 2005 but the world population increased by half a billion.

Limiting population by birth control seems to be the preferred method of most countries. Sterilization is the most widely practiced form of birth control in the U.S. and in the world. For men the procedure is vasectomy and in women it is tubal ligation.

Contraception is the preferred method of birth control for many who may want to have children at a later date. This falls under two categories: physical and chemical contraception. With physical methods of contraception the sperm is prevented from reaching the egg by such items as inter-uterine devices, condoms, diaphragms and cervical caps. With chemical contraception, sperm is killed or a woman is prevented from ovulating. This method uses items such as the pill, spermicidal creams, skin implants, vaginal foams and steroids.

At the U.N. Cairo Conference on Population (1994) discussions of birth control took place. Even though this meeting took place many years ago it still is a useful study since it brought forth attitudes that are prevalent but unpublicized today.

Many plans were discussed. The Roman Catholic Church and many Islamic nations objected to much of the discussion focusing on family planning and rights of women. The Roman Catholic Church believes in only the natural rhythm method of family planning. That is, no artificial means of preventing the sperm from reaching the egg is acceptable. If the couple involved do not want to have children they calculate fertile periods by watching the menstruation dates of the woman. Half- way between these dates is the fertile period, usually 13 days after a woman begins menstruation. American Catholics, as a group, generally practice methods that are not church approved forms of birth control.

At the Cairo Conference statistics were distributed indicating the use of contraception by women in various countries. Some of these were (in percent) France 80, Sweden 78, South Korea 77, U.S. 74, China 71, Thailand 66, Japan 64, Peru 59, Mexico 53, Egypt 47, India 45, Zimbabwe 43, Chile 43, Kenya 33, Iran 23, Pakistan 12. Researchers concluded that more women would use contraceptives if they were available.

Scientists measure the population-land ratio by carrying capacity which is the maximum number of individuals of any species that can be supported over a long term by an ecosystem. Once the carrying capacity is reached, countries should try to attain zero population growth. This is a theoretical goal rather than a realistic one. Infinite growth in a finite system is impossible. Each day we get closer to the absolute limits of growth.

There are many reasons couples have large families. One very strong reason is cultural acceptability. People in many cultures have become used to large families. They continue to support this culture dictate even though the relation between poverty and population is evident to them.

More children are born to cultures where there is a lack of reliable contraception available. More than 90 percent of the women of Nigeria said they would use contraception if it were available.

When my married friends Joe and Peg visited her Irish roots Joe was shocked when he could not buy condoms in that country at that time..

In many cultures, men consider it unmanly to use condoms and the pressure on birth control is shifted to women. This is particularly true in Latin America and Africa.

The more education parents have, the less likely they are to have large families . Education also influences family income and those who have less children in a given area are better off financially.

Children, in the work force, are another factor in lesser developed countries. In countries such as Indonesia, Malaysia and Burma girls as young as twelve years old are employed in clothing factories. They are slaves in our modern world. Boys and girls as young as ten years old are employed in weaving enterprises in many central Asian countries.

As people migrate to urban areas they tend to have fewer children. Back on the farm children are an asset, in the city they are not productive and are mouths to feed. On the farm they can feed chickens, work on crops and bring in the cows. Older people can take care of many farm duties. In the city, old and young people are wards of those aged in-between.

The cost of educating and raising a child enters into family planning. Malthus believed that people should never have children unless they can prove that they can support them. It takes about five thousand dollars to raise a child for the first year in the United States. Throw-away diapers alone will cost $700 the first year.

Education in many areas such as Latin America is considered necessary and many parents make unbelievable sacrifices to send their children to elementary school. In Africa, more than eighty percent of women never attend school. At the Cairo Conference mentioned previously, the status of women in the world was given high priority. If women are employed and educated they will have fewer children.

Infant mortality rates have decreased worldwide but many cultures continue to have the same number of children per family unit as in previous ages. Seventy years ago it was common for one out of three children in lesser developed countries to die before the age of ten. People in these regions tried to have many children in hopes that some of them will make it to adulthood. As adults they would help to support their aging parents. Even though infant mortality has declined, some people seem to feel that it is still necessary to have large families. Some countries have reversed this trend. In 1965 the average woman in Thailand had 6.3 children. In 1987, the number had dropped to 2.2 Significant drops in fertility have occurred in China, Cuba, Indonesia and Tunisia.

Average marriage age has some influence on family size. This is assuming women do not have children before they marry. This is not the situation in the United States. In most countries marrying at a young age produces more children per family and marrying at a later time produces fewer children.

The average age a women is married in Ireland is 26 and a man is 32. In the United States it is 23 for women and 26 for men. In China, the government has recommended the Rule of 52. A man and woman contemplating marriage should have a combined age of 52 or more. China gives many incentives to couples that have only one child. They get first choice of government jobs, housing and food. This one child policy has led to the killing of many girl babies since Chinese men consider it unmanly not to have a son. When the Chinese government started executing parents who kill their newborn daughters, the policy alleviated infanticide. Many people living in China West violate this one child policy without intervention since the government would like more buffer people in those areas.

When one considers the one child policy it is a shocking culture movement. It eliminates the terms brother, sister, cousin, uncle, and aunt.

Abortion is another method of limiting populations. Abortion occurs when a pregnancy is terminated before coming to term and the fetus is killed. There are an estimated 150,000 abortions a day worldwide. These are mostly in Lesser Developed Countries formerly called Third World Countries.

Family planning would eliminate the need for most abortions. In many countries such as most of those in Latin America, abortion is not legal. However, the abortion rate in many Latin American countries is higher than in places where abortion is legal. Roman Catholic Italy usually has the highest abortion rates in Europe.

The United States Supreme Court ruled that during the first three months of pregnancy abortion cannot legally be prevented by states. About one and a half million legal abortions are performed in the United States each year. About twenty percent of Americans believe abortions should be illegal. The confrontation between abortion proponents (Pro Choice) and abortion foes (Pro Life) has caused much hardship for both sides. The situation is heading toward a serious climax with Pro Life forces beginning to use terrorist tactics to shut down abortion clinics. There are about two thousand such clinics in the United States. However, the number is dwindling.

Migration of People

When conditions deteriorate for people they usually look about for more opportunity elsewhere. They migrate to other countries if they can be accepted. Many people migrate to these countries whether they are accepted or not. Recent history has seen thousands of people from Latin America and Asia crossing the United States border illegally. Many people consider legal immigration as well as illegal immigration as the biggest threat to the economic and social health of the United States.

Only a handful of countries will accept immigrants. Most countries are very protective of their borders. Some set up military units to either kill or frighten illegal immigrations.

There are about twenty million people fleeing their homelands every year in search of a place to live. Most of these are the result of wars or ethnic intimidation. More than half the population of Afghanistan was displaced in the recent wars there. Almost all of them have moved into Pakistan and Iran. These countries will tolerate them up to a point and then they will have to move elsewhere.

Refugees are people who flee their country because of fear of political, religious, or ethnic persecution or war. Today there are about four million refugees living in Europe, one million in Latin America and six million in the Middle East. The thousands of people living in camps for displaced peoples in Africa at this time can be added to the refugee problems of that continent.

The big movement of people, however, has been from rural to urban areas. Cities around the world are growing at an alarming rate as people abandon the land and look for a better life in cities, usually the capital cities of their country.

Migration to cities has led to the development known as the supercity or megacity. This is a city with a population of over ten million. Consider what it takes to get water, food, housing, clothing, medical care, trash pick-up, sewage disposal and electricity to such a place. It is mind boggling. Everything has to be brought in since the city is dependent on other places for its sustenance.

A good definition of the areal limits of supercity is based on its activities or function. Generally, one of the criteria in classification is the furthest distance a worker in the city is willing to commute.

Cities are population clusters of continuous built-up areas with the city boundary as the core. In this definition New York City would enter into New Jersey.

Present supercities would take in (order of largest populations) Tokyo, Mexico City, Sao Paulo, Seoul, New York, Bombay (old name), Osaka, Calcutta, Rio de Janeiro, Tehran, Buenos Aries, Cairo, Jakarta, Lagos, Manilla, Delhi, Karachi, Los Angeles and Moscow.

People migrate to cities for many reasons including employment, housing, medical care and social programs. In their villages these may not be available.

If the city does not readily accept the newcomers they move into shantytowns on the outskirts of the city. One half of Mexico City's population of thirty million lives in cardboard and tin shacks hastily constructed along with pieces of plastic and packing crates. On the outskirts of Manila in the Philippines three thousand people live on and in a garbage dump.

These shantytowns or slums have no sewage, no trash pick-up, no running water, no electricity and no police protection. People here live in fear of the day when the city decides it no longer can tolerate them When these people do get jobs they are at low wages and often hazardous to health. People who get these jobs find themselves trapped. They make enough money to live on and they can't risk going back to their villages where conditions are even worse.

A nation can alleviate migration to the city from rural areas by offering social services such as schools and immunization services in rural areas. Building new factories in rural settings will not only employ rural people but decrease pollution in the city. Creating working committees in rural areas who can determine the problems and their correction would be a move in the right direction. This would help eliminate the fear of the central authorities, prevalent in most rural areas.

The definition of a city has expanded from just that of its political boundaries to that of metropolitan area where everyone on the outskirts of the city are dependent upon the city for services and employment. Some geographers argue that the area from Boston to Washington D.C. is one city separated by green belts. This continuation of urbanization has been given names such as Megalopolis and Bosnywash.

Future Considerations

The United States does not have an official population policy. Should a nation have such a policy? One can see official posters in China advocating one child and in India two children. Even though we do not have an official policy we affect the population conditions in other countries by giving foreign aid, food relief and settlement of refugees.

We have legislation in the United States which, to some extent, promotes certain policies affecting population. For instance, we give tax exemptions for dependents of the taxpayer. This encourages larger families.

We subsidize construction of roads, sewer lines, water lines and airports which encourages excess city populations to move to the suburbs. This in turn encourages the destruction of forests, farm lands and wetlands.

One of the controversial issues in the United States is the lack of control over our borders. Many groups have taken up this cause. Two of the more vocal are *Zero Population Growth* and *Population Environment Balance.* both based in Washington D.C. Their philosophy is that although regions of the U.S. have wide open space it is not possible to locate people there because the carrying capacity of the land has already been reached and in most cases exceeded. The best way to get the land-people ratio stabilized is to limit immigration. Some other groups point to this seemingly idle land and encourage more immigration but when immigrants are permitted to enter the country most of them settle in the urban areas of California, Florida, New York and Texas, already our most populous states.

During the presidency of Jimmy Carter there was an agreement with the Cuban government that we would take their citizens who wished to come to the United States. We were overwhelmed with them. Premier Castro pulled a fast one and emptied his prisons and other institutions, putting the people on the boats to the United States. Our immigration service documented them and managed to find places for them throughout the country. In less than a year all of these people made their way to Florida and settled there. The criminals were especially dangerous and many of them ended up in U.S. prisons.

Another area of concern is our involvement in the population of foreign countries. Many people, including some influential legislators believe that when we send help in the form of medicines and food to needy countries, it only serves to increase their populations and these countries seem to have no sense of responsibility.

Years ago, an editorial in *Bioscience, Feb.* 1969 stated this philosophy when it said "We give food to the malnourished populations of the world that cannot or will not take very substantial measures to control their own reproductive rates" and this is "inhuman, immoral and irresponsible."

Regardless of your feelings about the subject, in the time it took to read this chapter the population of the world increased by 6,200 people.

Top ten supercities of the world and their populations. If each person requires one and a half pounds of food per day and 18 gallons of water, how much of each commodity would have to be delivered to a small city of 100,000 people? How much is needed for New York City in one day? The cities listed below have millions of people in their service areas. They do not produce food.

Supercities in order of population numbers in millions. 2008.

1. Tokyo.34.4 (2) Jakarta 21.8. (3) New York 20.0 (4) Manila 19.6 (5) Mumbai (Bombay) 19,5 (6) Sao Paulo 19.1 (7) Mexico City 18.4 (8) Delhi 18.0 (9) Osaka 17.3 (10) Cairo 16.7

FUTURE PROSPECTS

Present trends has some implications for the future. In the United States more members of the middle class are sinking into poverty. The population of the middle class is declining, poor people are increasing and more affluent (rich) people are getting more affluent.

Since 1980 (Reagan Years) the standard of living for the American family has been declining at the rate of four percent per year. There were more people living below the poverty line in 1995 than in the entire history of the country. There were more people unemployed in 1995 than during the Great Depression. In July 2011 the unemployed, those people collecting unemployment and registered for jobs was over ten percent of the work force. We are still the most envied country around the world but that status is rapidly eroding.

Most poor countries have high population increases. This results in migration to other regions. Even newly industrialized countries have population increases beyond the carrying capacity of their lands. Our neighbors are sneaking across our borders in larger numbers every year and putting stress on our social service agencies. In 2009 more than a thousand people a day made illegal crossing of our border from Mexico. About ten years ago more than a hundred thousand Haitians came to Florida in make-shift boats. At that time more than fifty thousand Cubans entered our country illegally. Boatloads of potential Chinese immigrants floundered and were rescued on both the Atlantic and Pacific coasts. They were given refugee status. This immigration, legal and illegal, coupled with our modest fertility rate will double the United States population in less than fifty years.

We have roughly 310 million people in the United States and by the year 2050 we could have over 500 million. This gives us a very short period of time in which to **double** our social services, our schools, our water supplies, our medical services, our food resources, our sewage systems and everything else necessary to our standard of living.

No one who considers the situation can deny that our quality of life is diminishing. Most thinking people will agree that our population has already reached, if not exceeded, the carrying capacity of the environment. This is true with most countries of the world.

What is our obligation to the rest of the world? Can we continue to accept immigrants as we have done in the past? Most countries have stopped immigration altogether and only the United States, Germany, Canada and Australia still accept other peoples in large numbers. Recently Germany has enacted legislation to halt the influx of foreigners, mostly refugees from war zones.

With no increase in productivity and a doubling of our population we will simply have to accept less out of life. We can look forward to energy shortages, exhausted land, scarce water and a radical change in our diets. Our lands are already at the limit of production and crop yield increases are not going to keep up with the population growth. We will no longer have the luxury of exporting food.

The basis for our farm productivity is petroleum. We will run out of domestic petroleum supplies in twenty years and foreign sources will most likely hang on to their limited supplies. We are losing farm acres to urbanization at the rate of about 2 million acres a year. Most "thinking" countries of the world have limited the development on arable land. The United States mentality seems to think that it is the individual's right in a free society to do what one wants with private property.

Today, the average American spends about fifteen percent of income on food. In Europe and Japan the figure is thirty percent and in Lesser Developed Countries the cost runs from fifty to a hundred percent of one's income.

The hope for our future depends on legislation and regulation enacted by the United States Congress. Eventually they will be forced to recognize the desperate needs of our future and we can only hope sensible legislation which limits the profit motive as a consideration is enacted.

We must limit our population growth and wasteful use of our resources. We must treasure our water, air and soil. We must conserve, practice sustained yield and recycle.

At the beginning of 2011 there were over fifty wars in progress. Most of these were not reported in the American press. We heard about Afghanistan, Chechen, Iraq, Tajikistan, Rwanda and Somalia. We heard very little about the wars in Mexico, Peru, Ecuador, Sri Lanka, Cambodia, the Philippines and Indonesia where intense fighting was carried on. The present drug war in Mexico has resulted in over a million deaths in the last four years.

Most of these wars were over resources and a major resource was water. In this country, skirmishes are shaping up over resources of land and water. The burgeoning population centers of Southern California have already exceeded the carrying capacity of the land. Groups of citizens living in Northern California have organized to break free of the south. How far these ideas will go largely depends on stress factors.

Los Angeles already transports most incoming water over three hundred miles. It uses about nine billion gallons of fresh water a day. Its population will double in about fifteen years. Where will it get the extra nine billion gallons of water EACH DAY?

The international community has many organized meetings to discuss the implications of population, food, refugees, health and resources. Not much has been accomplished at these meetings and most countries favored their own agendas. However, what has been accomplished is the understanding that there are problems that have to be solved and most of these have to be solved on the international level.

THE EARTH SUMMIT - Brazil 1992

The most acclaimed international meeting the world has ever seen was held in Rio de Janeiro, Brazil in June of 1992. It was the United Nations Earth Summit on the environment which hosted delegates from 178 nations including 116 heads of state.

The world expected the United States to lead the way into an environmental awareness that would have far reaching effects well into the 21st century. Instead, the United States, under the leadership of President George Bush I, had a negative impact on the proceedings.

The United States insisted that carbon dioxide emission standards be eliminated from the wording of the global warming treaty. At the time of the treaty the United States with 5% of the world's people produced 23% of the world's industrial carbon dioxide.

The United States position was that the wording of the" greenhouse gas" emission treaty was too strict in its first draft and pushed for a useless high-sounding document which eventually let any nation oversee its own emissions. President Bush said his "obligation is to protect American jobs as well as the environment".

A biodiversity treaty was completely opposed by the United States and President Bush refused to sign the final draft. The treaty set aside important habitat areas in order to save and preserve diverse species. President Bush said that it would require additional U.S. aid to poor countries and would harm America's biotechnology industry.

The message from the developing countries was that they cannot afford to preserve their natural resources such as rainforests until their economies are improved by foreign aid. Without foreign aid they are forced to proceed with resource exploitation for their own economic survival.

Japan paved the way to the future when its Prime Minister Kiichi Miyazawa pledged $7.7 billion in environmental aid to developing nations. He stated that Japan would also eliminate the use of all CFCs in three years and reduce its carbon dioxide emissions to 1990 levels by the year 2000. Japan emerged as the environmental leader of the world. **Note:** Japan did do this.

It may be noted that at the time of the Summit, Japan fishing fleets still hunted whales, businesses still traded in endangered species and Japanese lumber imports were responsible for destruction of large tracts of tropical and temperate forests.

Basically, the main tenets of the Rio meeting were vague and the spirit of the meeting was its strong point. In the brief ten days, the world focused on the environment and perhaps in the future, all countries will be sensitive to the issues outlined at the meeting.

INTERNATIONAL CONFERENCE ON POPULATION AND DEVELOPMENT 1994

Cairo, Egypt was the meeting site for the International Conference on Population and Development sponsored by the United Nations. It was assumed by the sponsors that cooperation in limiting population and increasing opportunities for poor countries would be the agenda. However, differences in culture became evident and opinions on how to improve the lot of most of the world differed.

Although the main topic was population it was mostly about the rights of women. The original draft proposals called for a full range of reproductive and health-care services, including contraceptives and sex education for women. The organizers believed that the equality of women was the cornerstone of any population program.

The premise seemed simple enough, "what happens to a woman should be her decision". This might have been fine for most western cultures in highly developed nations but applied to other cultures it was an explosive issue.

Some Muslim clerics, from countries where women are hidden by veils and where the Koran's teachings are the law of the land, were outraged at the idea of equality for women. The agenda was an attack on their culture.

Giving the Islamic protests extra support was the Vatican led by Pope John Paul II. He accused the United Nations of trying to establish a worldwide right to abortion and demeaning the importance of the family. Catholic priests attacked the draft program for allegedly encouraging homosexuality and adolescent sex.

The American delegation was led by Vice President Albert Gore who was recognized around the world as a concerned environmentalist. He and his staff were convinced that population limitation is the world's central issue.

The American's pointed to Thailand as an example. Thirty years ago it was a poverty stricken country. Its government began to stress the importance of women's health and education. Female literacy increased to 90 percent. The average number of babies born to each woman decreased from six in 1968 to 2.1 in 1994.

Many interesting statistics were presented at the meeting. For instance, of the 960 million illiterate adults in the world, two thirds are women. Of the 130 million children denied elementary education 90 million are girls. Women are legally beaten almost everywhere.

Food per capita is falling around the world and the population continues to increase. Raising the status of women seems to be a way to counteract the dilemma. It is a tragedy that in many areas of the world women are treated as property rather than as an integral part of humanity.

On a personal note, I gag when I attend a wedding and the official in charge asks "Who gives this woman to this man?"

In most areas of the world there are more people than the environment can support. This leads to poverty which leads to destruction of the environment. Each region has a carrying capacity and when this capacity is exceeded, extreme measures must be implemented in order for the population to survive. Food and other resources must be imported or some of the population must move out. If this cannot be accomplished, the usual result is war.

Many environmentalists believe the population of the United States has reached its carrying capacity and we are already importing many resources to compensate for the excess population. For more and more Americans, the standard of living continues to diminish. Today, there are more Americans living below the poverty level than in the entire history of the country. Despite this statistic, we are still better off than most of the world.

We became the world leader through exploitation of our natural resources, our soils, water and forests. Today, these resources are at a critical stage and we must conserve them, recycle them and practice sustainable use. Most of all - we must change our lifestyles.

IX CONTROVERSY

The Tea Party

The Tea Party, as the group is called, is really not a nationally organized group but a reference to many groups who place themselves under that label. The different groups collectively are recognized as politically conservative and in some instances libertarian since Ron Paul has had some influence on their organizations. Basically, the different Tea Party groups agree on reduction of the national debt, reduction of the federal budget deficit and a reduction of federal spending. Other loosely defined goals are a stricter interpretation of the United States Constitution and curtailment of immigration..

The Tea Party can be compared to any protest group with an ax to grind. They started to get organized shortly after the election of President Obama and gained adherents when there was talk of tax increases.

The Tea Party movement has caucuses in the House of Representatives and the Senate of the United States. At this time there are no leaders of the "party" who can assist in developing a platform and an agenda. They are simply people angry with the present government and wish to display this anger. Several candidates for the House of Representatives have exploited this anger in order to be elected.

Most, if not all, of the candidates backed by Tea Party groups have been Republican which gives rise to the charge that they are simply a new wing of the Republican Party. A Washington Post poll in October 2010 found 87% of people who claimed to be with the Tea Party as discontented with the Republicans in office and they wished to replace them with different Republicans.

One of the causes that the not-organized Tea Party opposed was the universal health care bill of 2010. Below is a recap of some of the salient points of the bill and the opposition. Passage of the bill was an indication that the Tea Party has not yet reached sufficient strength to influence significant legislation.

Bruce

Bruce is a long-time friend and regular correspondent of mine. He and I took trips to Mexico and Russia as well as over the United States. He learned to speak Spanish while in college by using a short wave radio every evening. He became so proficient in Spanish he often passed for a native in South America. He taught a year in Puerto Rica in the language.

Bruce is twenty years my junior but we have much in common except politics. He and I founded the Mother Earth Society which never quite took off but has some ardent members.

Bruce and I have divergent views on politics and the role of government and we discuss this often in our correspondence. I believe his views would be to the right of Pat Toomey. A few letters ago I asked Bruce what he considered to be the exact role of the federal government. Here are excerpts from his letter of 29 August 2011, with his permission.

"Federal Government in our affairs: national military defense including international borders, standardizing the system of weights and measures which should be metric, supervising a standard monetary system which should be based on gold, some involvement in interstate commerce to prevent monopolies (that would include transportation, but not the construction and maintenance of highways, airports, harbors, railroads, which can be done privately and through tolls). That is about it. Government need not be involved in education, health, welfare, postal, parks and recreation, environmental, space exploration, insurance, unemployment compensation, cash for clunkers, ad infinitum. Maybe some involvement in pure food and drug standards, but that is included in the weights and measure and commerce anti-monopoly issues previously mentioned."

He goes on about Hurricane Irene and other items of interest to us. Then he remembers to add some things. "You really have it figured out where you mention in your essay the seriousness of overpopulation. That is essentially the cause of all our problems, environmental, inflation, unemployment, psychological problems, infectious diseases."

Later again in the letter: "Another thing government should be involved in would be a justice system to permit rule of law involving fundamentals of our existence, not whether you can smoke in a restaurant or not. Just remember that every law takes away personal freedom. Same for taxes taking away freedom to spend your hard earned money as you desire. As the USA goes forward from 1776 we have lost a tremendous amount of personal freedom. That continues today, I remember in 1967 when I bought my first rifle for $18.00. I just walked into ACE Auto on S. Main St in Washington PA and bought it. No problem. Now it takes one hour of paperwork and the sale can even be denied by a glitch in records."

"Another problem is poor obedience and enforcement of present laws. That leads to passage of new laws to cover the old laws. That leads back to overpopulation which leads to trying to have a cop behind every tree. Rule of law should be strict and decisive. Crooked lawyers twist those circumstances to favor their lucre. "

The Health Care Debate

A brief government description of the so called Obamacare Bill states "The Affordable Care Act, passed by Congress and signed into law by the President in March 2010, gives you better health security by putting in place comprehensive health insurance reforms that hold insurance companies accountable, lower health care costs, guarantee more choice, and enhance the quality of care for all Americans."

There is no doubt that America need universal health care legislation that will put the "free enterprise" health care system into some sort of normal affordable channels. The recent health care bill seems to be conservative even though it was passed by liberal Democrats and opposed by conservative Republicans. There was no room for compromise which in the past has been the essence of good legislation enacted in this country. With forty five million citizens without health care insurance one would think sensible legislators would want to lower that statistic. Anyway, it is a beginning and it will remain a law even though the conservative "talking head" industry tries to whip up their constituency into a frenzy. Their listeners can't seem to make the leap from their rhetoric to their bank accounts.

The latest health care legislation expands coverage to most of the uninsured and protects those who already have insurance. In a few years, with this legislation, about 95% of Americans will have some sort of health care coverage. Don't thank Republicans, they were opponents of Social Security and Medicare as well as hundreds of other progressive social legislation.

Fred says "it's all socialism." Well Fred when more than fifty percent of our citizens are employed by the federal and state governments and another twenty percent relies on government aid I would say you are fighting a lost cause if you are against socialism. I might point out that Fred's main income in his lifetime has been through working for government owned enterprises.

A negative aspect of the legislation is the mandating of health insurance without a public option to keep the insurance companies honest. Insurance companies and their agents rank right up there with used car salesmen. The bill offers subsidies for people who can't afford to buy health care insurance. The bill should have taken health care out of the hands of "for profit" medical industries, but it didn't.

There is also funding for community health centers which will be an asset to people living in rural areas. It will also end discrimination against people with preexisting conditions. It will add more money to help states pay for an expansion of Medicaid for poor people. "But, this is socialism," cries Fred as he goes to pick up his unemployment check in West Virginia.

The legislation unfortunately restricts reproductive rights of women. It also opens the door to unfair costs for women in reference to their simply being women with what are termed "woman's problems." Also, undocumented workers will not be able to benefit from the legislation since they will be sent back to their place of origin if they try to get in on it..

Once again the legislation gives a blank check to the pharmaceutical industry. The no collective bargaining facet of the legislation to bring down government costs of pharmaceuticals should have made the recalcitrant Republicans vote for the measure with grinning expressions. But, they were more interested in "getting Obama" than in the welfare of Americans or they would have endeavored to compromise on the legislation that was almost certain to pass.

A recap of the bill: it bans lifetime limits of expenditure, it bans dropping coverage when the person needs it most, it helps cover young adults on their parent's health plans, it prohibits discrimination against children with pre-existing conditions and it restricts the use of annual limits.

Food Stamps

A few years ago, in my food store, I looked at some red grapes imported from Chile and decided I would not pay the asking price since we were watching our expenditures and were on a budget. The woman in front of me had three packs of them in her cart. When she went to pay for her groceries she did so with food stamps. This is the kind of situation that the "right wing of society" likes to bandy about. I tried not to curse under my breath about the waste of government money but decided the shopper needed some lessons in frugality or was unable to make a connection with her need for food stamps and her lifestyle.

Years ago before food stamps the government was giving away cans of beef, pounds of butter and five pound boxes of cheese to indigents. My alcoholic neighbor with four kids would sell these in order to finance his habits of cigarets and beer. Perhaps, I should have cut him some slack since he was a former U.S. Marine who had seen hand-to-hand combat in the islands of the Pacific. I could not resist the urge to shake my head.

One recent email forwarded to me said "instead of food stamps the needy people should get a sack of rice from the government and told to learn to live with it.
As a conservationist I had to agree that it was possible for a person

to live on a five hundred pound sack of rice for a year. Besides, I had met someone who had done it. He was a Taiwan immigrant who had been given a library job in Michigan many years ago. He lived on one bowl of rice a day for six years and saved his money since he wanted what America had to offer. He spiked up the rice with vegetables given to him by friends and often he would mix an egg in with his rice. He would buy things like plastic pandas from Taiwan and resell them to markets in the states. When I met him twenty five years after he came to this country he was a millionaire. He imported his brother who had three children and a wife and they set up a restaurant business in Indiana, not far from the Notre Dame campus. It was a real success story if there ever was one. Oriental immigrants are the most successful of the immigrant groups in America. I have met at least fifty of them and they are certainly self- disciplined and self- reliant. Say what you will about Communist China, but I never met a Chinese who wasn't a capitalist at heart.

Back to food stamps. The county where I live has a population of 204,000. The number of people in the county receiving food stamps is 37% of the population. If this percentage is true across the country then there are over a hundred million people receiving food stamp aid. How can we get the people back to work at a decent livable wage? The problem is easier to see than it is to solve. Since our representatives are not trained in the solution of these problems they should engage people who are instead of political hacks of their own party.

When people have nothing, they have nothing to lose. If programs such as food stamps are taken away from them then logically they are a threat to the stability of society.

The Resources requirement for food stamps is that a household cannot have more than $2000 in resources. If the household includes a person 60 or older or who is disabled the limit is $3000. Resources of people who receive Supplemental Security income or benefits under the Temporary Assistance for Needy Families program are not counted for food stamp purposes. Resources include cash, bank accounts and other property.

A home and the land it is on will not count against the household as a resource category. The thinking here is that the situation is only temporary and food stamps will help the recipients get over the hump of low income. A vehicle counts differently from one situation to the next depending on the use of the vehicle.

Most households must also include an income limit. Certain things do not count as income and can be subtracted from the income total. Income limits vary by household size and may change from year to year.

Going back to the premise of actions based on a hereditary instinct for survival we can see in those people who criticize the food stamp program a feeling that "someone is getting away with something and somehow something is being taken from me." In the extension of the philosophy that may be true, but shouldn't those of us who are fortunate not to have to resort to food stamps be willing to give up a little of our good fortune to those who are needy?

Ethnic and Racial Considerations

Many demonstrations in the United States have been along ethnic, sexual, cultural and racial lines as well as against legislation designed to benefit or hinder these groups. Some discussion might help in understanding some of this. **Pointing out that there is no difference in DNA of all humans, regardless of skin color, probably would fall on deaf ears of the prejudiced.** Unfortunately many of our legislators are closet bigots who need unmasked. However, being a bigot can easily propel one to office in certain districts of the country.

"Help Wanted – Irish Need Not Apply" was a sign in many Boston and New York windows about a hundred and fifty years ago after the influx of Irish immigrants to America as the result of the famine caused by the failure of the potato crop in Ireland. The Irish immigrants outwitted their adversaries by increasing their numbers and, by doing this ,seizing political power in many areas. Eventually, the Irish Cop and his authority became the standard stereotype in American literature and entertainment

My former student Hideo was a Japanese graduate student who came to America on a student visa. He enrolled in a university in Texas when he first came here. The color of his skin was a shade darker than light brown. On his first day on campus he went to the cafeteria, filled his tray with food, walked out to the passageway that led to the seating area and came to two dining areas. The dining area on the left was filled with all black students and the one on the right was filled with only white students. He said he stood there for what seemed like eternity and didn't know which one to enter. One of the white students saw his predicament and told him to join his group. Hideo eventually transferred to my college and we had many discussions about the various cultural differences between his country and mine.

In 1998 a study of young black men between the ages of 18 and 26 indicated that one out of three of them were either in prison, on parole, awaiting trial or had already been in prison and released. There were many theories on this situation. It seemed that the theories could be broken down into (1) young black men were criminally oriented and (2) young black men were victims of the social and financial structure of our society. Unemployment statistics were used to support the latter.

In my city of Erie Pennsylvania almost all homicides are committed within the ethnic groups. One might conclude from that situation that ethnic or racial discrimination was not responsible for the crime. But, how about legislation concerning unemployment, social services, health care and education which might stimulate animosity within a group? Nationwide the category labeled white make up 84% of the population but are victims of 82% of crime. Blacks make up 12% of the population and make up 15 % of the victims. Whites make up 81% of the population today but will make up 73 % by 2050 if the birthrates hold. Blacks make up 13 % today but will make up 16 % by 2050. Whatever category Latinos are in, they will be the largest minority ethnic group in America by 2050. Depending on how you measure Latinos, they may already be there. Also, there is much interracial cohabitation and it would be difficult to put the offspring into a white or black category.

When President Lyndon Johnson signed his first civil rights legislation into law he said in so many words, "After I sign this bill the Democrats will lose The South." He was correct on that score and the Republicans won The South on thinly disguised prejudicial rhetoric rather than on the party platform. They hold much of The South today with a hint of prejudice toward blacks and Hispanics. Their attempts to draw these two groups into their party have not met with success.

The culmination of the prejudice came in the Bush-Gore election when more than 15,000 blacks were disenfranchised. Although they were registered voters their names were not submitted to their various voting districts. Had they been able to vote we would not have had George W. Bush as president. Where was the Supreme Court? They were busy making sure Florida did not complete their recount of the close election votes. What ever happened to states right's?

Historically, there are recognized multiple origins for ethnic hatred and the resulting ethnic conflicts. In some societies, like the Middle East and Africa, it is rooted in tribalism, while in others it originates from a history of non-peaceful co-existence of neighbors and the resulting actual disputed issues.

Often ethnic conflict is enhanced by nationalism and feeling of national superiority. For which reason feelings of hatred across the border combines with prejudice.

Ethnic conflict may stem from the feeling of real or perceived discrimination by another ethnic group, such as occurred in Bosnia with the Serbians.

Ethnic and political hatred has often been exploited and even fueled by some political leaders to serve their agenda of seeking to consolidate the nation or gain an electorate by calling for a united struggle against a common real or imaginary enemy. This was illustrated when many Japanese-Americans who were loyal to the United States were interred in "holding" camps during World War II.

In many countries incitement to ethnic or racial hatred is a criminal offense. This is true in Great Britain, Germany and somewhat in the United States.

Racial discrimination differentiates between individuals on the basis of real and perceived racial and physical differences, and has been the official government policy in several countries, such as South Africa in the colonial era, and in many states of the USA. The racial and ethnic legislation and studies of Nazi Germany are well documented. The Jews were the main group attacked by the Nazi Government Jews were the historic scapegoats of history. We as a nation think we are not prejudiced, then every once in a while some celebrity will lash out and remind us that we are not pure at heart.

During the Bush-Kerry election campaigns I listened to talk radio on my way to and from work. On one broadcast, the leading talking head at that time mentioned Kerry's Jewish grandfather eighteen times in the half hour it took me to get to work. That same "host" made remarks about Jesse Jackson's tears when President Obama was elected. No matter what one thinks of Jesse Jackson, he earned those tears. He was and is a tireless worker for civil rights and has put his life on-the-line many times for this cause.

There is a cycle of discrimination and prejudice that somehow needs to be broken. The cycle may start against a group that has been disadvantaged. On the basis of this the idea is implanted that the disadvantaged is inferior to the majority group. This creates renewed discrimination and prejudice theories which justify the inferior position of the disadvantaged group.

The advantaged group may believe that the disadvantaged blame society and other groups because they are inferior and therefore they have not succeeded in getting their share of the resources. Other groups and individuals may actually believe that they are superior to the disadvantaged. They often discount their advantages as being pure luck and imagine their position of advantage is due to their personal skills and integrity. Their success might be from inheritance of wealth or position.

Elite groups may foster prejudices in order to divide the disadvantaged groups into smaller units in order to keep control. Play the Florida Cubans against the Haitians and native Blacks.

If there is one thing certain it is that people learn prejudice and it is practiced from the standpoint of the survival instinct. According to a study by the Mayo Clinic children learn stereotyping around age four. By age seven their prejudices have been established. They recommend that parents don't tolerate ethnic jokes, answer the child's questions directly, for instance, skin color is based on melanin and provide children with interaction activities. Teach tolerance. Oh yes, and get an inventory and handle on your own prejudices.

Legislation that will help to defuse protesting, prejudice and discrimination would be hate crime legislation, forced school busing and educational opportunity as well as affirmative action. These won't stop prejudice but at least it will force America's intolerance into a reflective spotlight.

Government Employees and Strikes

Employees of the federal (and state) governments should hae no legal right to strike or bring a lawsuit against the government. They are a part of the government and therefore an arm of the government cannot logically sue the government or bring some part of its operation to a standstill. Negotiation yes, strike or lawsuit no.

In times of financial stress salaries could logically be lowered as well as raised. To pay off a large debt, a one day reduction in salary, say by ten percent, for all wages of those employed with the government by made.

Salaries of the federal legislature should be certified as a voting referendum. The salaries of Representatives could be up for a vote every two years and those for the senate every six years. That way there would be no adjustments from year to year. A candidate would know the salary exactly when he seeks office. It doesn't seem to matter what the salary is since millions of dollars more than the salary are spent on elections anyway.

No employee of the government should be able to sue the government. Arbitration seems to be some kind of myth. In my tenure as a school board member we went to arbitration eleven times and each time the board of arbitration came down in favor of the teachers. It was as if the Board was a branch of the Teacher's Association.

I am certainly in favor of the tenure laws in education, but it is up to those associations connected with it to police their own ranks. One semester a colleague assigned term papers the first class of the term and then canceled classes until the last week of the term. His procedure was upheld by a Committee of Arbitration even though he was not available on campus during that term.

There were many such instances in my college teaching career and I covered most of them in my book College Daze at Punxie.

Death Penalty

Capital punishment is an issue that needs rational rather than emotional discussion. We like to think that life is precious, and it is, but life is cheap in most parts of the world. Many people turn their backs daily on starvation, violence, and political executions without batting an eye.

In order to have a moral code concerning the legal taking of a life we must conclude that if a person commits murder then that person is willing and should sacrifice his own life. But, there is always a counter-argument to logic.

The Supreme Court of the United States has stated, "Indeed, the decision that capital punishment may be the appropriate sanction in extreme cases is an expression of the community's belief that certain crimes are themselves so grievous an affront to humanity that the only adequate response may be the penalty of death."

In discussing the issue we must ask is the purpose of the death penalty to (1) punish the criminal (2) deter others from committing a similar crime (3) remove someone from society who would be a constant threat to society (4) remove someone from society who is incapable of rehabilitation, and (5)

take retribution on behalf of the victim.

Capital punishment in the United States, in practice, applies only for aggravated murder and more rarely for felony murder. It appears that if you out-and-out kill someone you would not have to forfeit your own life, but if you add some sort of aggravation twist to the killing then your life is in jeopardy.

Capital punishment was always a penalty in common law for many felonies, and was enforced in all of the American colonies prior to the Declaration of Independence. Following the American Revolution the common law was maintained in the United States, capital punishment with it.

The methods of execution and the crimes subject to the penalty vary by jurisdiction and have varied widely throughout time, though today they are usually done by poisoning the criminal. There were 37 executions in the United States in 2008, the lowest number since 1994. (largely due to lethal injection litigation revolving around a now resolved constitutional question).There were 46 executions in 2010, 44 by lethal injection, one by electric chair in Virginia, and one by firing squad in Utah.

Capital punishment has often been a controversial social issue in the United States; while historically, a large majority of the American public has favored it in cases of murder. The extent of this support has varied over time, and there has long been strong opposition from some sectors of the population. While public support today is substantially lower than it was in the 1980s and '90s, it has been largely static over the past decade. Public support for execution reached an all time high of 80 percent in 1994.

A 2010 Gallop poll showed 64% of Americans favored the death penalty in cases of murder, while 29% opposed it. It should be noted that when life in prison without parole is listed as a poll option, the support for the death penalty drops; one 2001 poll showed 46% of Americans would prefer the death penalty and 45% would prefer life in prison.

Capital punishment is a controversial issue, with many prominent organizations and individuals participating in the debate. Amnesty International and some religious groups oppose capital punishment on moral grounds, while the Innocence Project works to free wrongly convicted prisoners, including death row inmates, based on newly available DNA tests. Other groups, such as the Southern

Baptists, law enforcement organizations, and some victims' rights groups support capital punishment.

The United States is one of only three industrialized democracies that still have it. Japan has recently executed murderers. South Korea currently has a moratorium in effect; in both countries, public support for the death penalty is high.

Elections have sometimes turned on the issue of the death penalty. In 1986, three justices were removed from the Supreme Court of California by the electorate partly because of their opposition to the death penalty. Religious groups are widely split on the issue of capital punishment, generally with more conservative groups likely to support it and more liberal groups likely to oppose it. Many groups are stalling for time by calling for a moratorium on the death penalty.

In October 2009, the American Law Institute voted to disavow the framework for capital punishment that it had created in 1962, as part of the Model Penal Code. "in light of the current intractable institutional and structural obstacles to ensuring a minimally adequate system for administering capital punishment." A study commissioned by the institute had said that experience had proved that the goal of individualized decisions about who should be executed and the goal of systemic fairness for minorities and others could not be reconciled.

In total, 138 prisoners have been either acquitted, or received pardons or commutations on the basis of possible innocence, since 1973. Death penalty opponents often argue that this statistic shows how perilously close states have come to undertaking wrongful executions, proponents point out that the statistic refers only to those exonerated in law, and that the truly innocent may be a smaller number. A recent court decision to release a mother who obviously killed her child received much public attention. The judge say he is going to write a book about it. Sensational trials have a way of turning into sensational best sellers.

Arguments for and against capital punishment are based on moral, practical, and religious grounds. Advocates of the death penalty argue that it deters crime, is a good tool for prosecutors in plea bargaining, improves the community by eliminating violent anti-socials, provides closure to surviving victims or loved ones, and is a just penalty for the crimes it punishes.

Opponents argue that the death penalty is not an effective means of deterring crime, risks the execution of the innocent, is unnecessarily barbaric in nature, is levied disproportionately upon men, racial minorities, and the poor, cheapens human life, and puts a government on the same base moral level as those criminals involved in murder.

Another argument is the cost. The convict is more likely to use the whole appeals process if the jury issues a death sentence than if it issues life without parole. But others who contest this argument say that the greater cost of appeals where the prosecution does seek the death penalty is offset by the savings from avoiding trial altogether in cases where the defendant pleads guilty to avoid the death penalty,

My comment: The cost of administering the death penalty is the result of legislation enacted by people whose livelihood before their election was made through their law offices. By complicating legislation they insure that their ilk will continue to prosper. Thomas Jefferson wrote on this subject many times, in effect, saying that if you want something screwed up then get a bunch of lawyers to work on it. My other comment is that lawyers are the scum of society until you need one.

As noted in the introduction to this segment, the American public has recently maintained its position of support for capital punishment for murder. However, when given a choice between the death penalty and life imprisonment without parole, support has traditionally been significantly lower than polling which has only mentioned the death penalty as a punishment; in a 2010 poll, for instance, the disparity narrowed, with 49% favoring the death penalty and 46% favoring life imprisonment. The highest level of support recorded overall was 80% in 1994 (16% opposed), and the lowest recorded was 42% in 1966 (47% opposed); on the question of the death penalty vs. life without parole, the strongest preference for the death penalty was 61% in 1997 with 29% favoring life, and the lowest preference for the death penalty was 47% in 2006 with 48% favoring life in prison.

Arguing against capital punishment, Amnesty International believes that "The death penalty is the ultimate denial of human rights. It is the premeditated and cold-blooded killing of a human being by the state in the name of justice. It violates the right to life. It is the ultimate cruel, inhuman and degrading punishment. There can never be any justification for torture or for cruel treatment."

There are some defendants who have earned the ultimate punishment our society has to offer by committing murder with aggravating circumstances present. Society has the duty to act in the defense of society. The death penalty assures society that the actor involved will no longer be able to threaten society. How many murderers were released after serving the minimum sentence and then committed murder again? George Bush I was partially elected on the Willie Horton issue where the actor was released from prison and in a short time committed another murder. The Republicans were so effective in their campaign I almost believed that the political opponent Michael Dukakis drove Willie Horton to Maryland where the murder was committed.

Catholic Cardinal McCarrick, Archbishop of Washington, writes "...the death penalty diminishes all of us, increases disrespect for human life, and offers the tragic illusion that we can teach that killing is wrong by killing."

The vast majority of democratic countries in Europe and Latin America have abolished capital punishment over the last fifty years. The United States and most democracies in Asia, and almost all totalitarian governments retain it. It is my opinion that the majority of Europeans are against the death penalty because they had seen it abused before World War II and the memories of this are still strong. Not many who lived through World War II are alive today, but the legacy and actions of that time are being kept alive through various organizations who do not want the public to forget.

Crimes that carry the death penalty vary greatly worldwide from treason and murder to theft. In military tribunals around the world, courts-martial have sentenced capital punishments also for cowardice, desertion, insubordination and mutiny. In the military history of the United States one soldier was executed for cowardice.

As of October 2009, capital punishment in the US is officially sanctioned by 34 states, as well as by the federal government. Each state with legalized capital punishment has different laws regarding its methods, age limits and crimes which qualify.

If you are going to kill someone and want to be assured that you won't give up your life and that you will have good food, medical benefits, enjoy television and be able to read and have a roof over your head then lure that someone to the following states which have no death penalty - Alaska, Hawaii, Iowa, Maine, Massachusetts, Michigan, Minnesota, New Jersey, New Mexico, New York, North Dakota, Rhode Island, Vermont, West Virginia, Wisconsin and the District of Columbia,

X THE SUMMING UP

The majority of Americans believe that the present government authorities are not capable of getting the country back-on-its-feet.

Should these authorities resign? One cynical way to look at it, is to say that if they did resign the state governors would only appoint political hacks from their own political party, instead of seeking out non-politicians with credentials to the task at hand. There might be some exceptions. One of the excellent appointments of this nature was made by Bush II when he appointed Robert Gates as Secretary of Defense.

The Legislative Branch of the country needs help for the benefit of the country from individuals and groups who must abandon their special interests for the sake of the country. Somehow the wealthy people in America have got to realize that they have some obligation and need some commitment to the welfare of the country that made them wealthy and sustains their wealth. There are many parallels in history, recent and ancient, that illustrates that the wealthy cannot maintain their wealth while ordinary citizens live in dire circumstances. We are fast approaching that condition in America.

One Parallel

Prior to the second century A.D. Wealthy Romans, especially the hyper-rich senatorial class, did practice "noblesse oblige." Ruthless and ambitious they were, but they also realized their wealth and position was inextricably linked to the fortunes of their empire. Being an officer in the Roman army, like Marc Anthony, was a source of wealth, power and privilege.

But beginning in the second century, the Roman ruling class turned inward and lost interest in the Empire. The majority of Roman officials now came from the "Barbarians" with some of them even becoming Roman emperors. The empire was divided in half with one capital in Rome and the other in Constantinople. This became unsustainable for the Empire, and that capital was finally moved to Ravenna. Wealthy Romans hoarded their wealth and retired to their country villas. You can actually see this shift in the archeological records.

This is not to give a history of the rise and fall of the Roman Empire but to remind everyone that **for any nation to survive, all of its citizens must actually care about it.** The bankers and speculators on Wall Street have lost sight of this, just like their wealthy Roman counterparts did two thousand years ago. And we know what happened next. (***Bonnie Henderson***)

We need a truly civil service government with salaried officials trained for the bureaucracy, hired by merit, disengaged from any private interest in the body they serve and accountable to some disinterested other body.

We have to assume there is some effort being made at the federal level to prune useless offices and to prevent the creation of more of them. The Czars appointed by President Obama come immediately to mind.

Clive Cook, a Brit writing in the *Financial Times* stated that Washington's dysfunction saps the promise of the country. He claims that America's ethic of strong work and self reliance is still strong. He believes the Constitution's checks and balances prevents inordinately strong influence by one of the trio. We could argue that is not quite true when we look at recent decisions by the Supreme Court and the takeover of several legislative activities by the Bush II Executive branch invading Congressional territory.

Cook refers to Congressional action as "noisy impotence" which is a pretty good assessment of the present situation. This do nothing strategy between competing factions in Congress can only result in decline. The U.S. needs immediate action on the health system, the tax system, immigration and education. So says Clive Cook and who among us will disagree with him, other than, perhaps members of Congress.

Last I checked the favorable opinion of Congress was at eighteen percent. When it was at twenty five percent a couple of years ago George Will asked, "Who are these twenty five percent?" He wondered how the opinion could be so high.

In other polls people seemed to favor their congressional representatives over the general representative. This is probably due to the smoozing applied in the home districts.

Unfortunately, the type of people who can win elections are not the type of people we really should have representing us. In order to win an election they have to resort to the most debasing strategies known to humankind. They have to prostitute themselves to their contributors and once elected many of them continue their prostitution in order to be reelected.

If we are to effect change then the majority of us have to give up membership and loyalty to a political party. The ranks of Independent should swell to fifty percent and the other fifty divided by the other parties. Regardless of ideology that loyalty to a political party has got to go. Neither major party in Congress deserves our loyalty anyway.

People might say that they want to belong to a political party so they can vote in the primary and have some influence on the choice of candidate. This might be a compromise but to this argument the answer is still No. .

Some states already allow Independents to vote for a party candidate in the primary. That seems to be a contradiction since the Political Party is a private club and only its members should have a vote as to whom their candidate will be. If Independents could vote then it would be possible to stack the deck for or against one party. Independents might be encouraged to vote Republican to keep someone who is not a party hack from winning the primary. The Republican Party might encourage Independents to vote in the Democrat Primary to elect a candidate they know they can beat in the general election. No, if Independents want a voice in the primary they should join a political party. Those who are truly independent will just have to accept their absence from the primary.

I thought of a system that could be used. If a person registers to vote he might be able to put down ID meaning he is registered as an Independent but wishes to vote in the Democrat Primary. IR would mean a vote in the Republican Primary. This designation could be changed every two years, but not anytime the person gets a hankering. Switching ID to Democrat or Republican could be made anytime before a primary election. Since this is a stupid idea it will be championed by a lot of people who read this.

Unemployment problem

Today, unemployment hovers around ten percent of the workforce. The actual figure is probably closer to fifteen percent. When marginally employed people are considered the numbers are probably close to twenty percent. I have searched diligently and have not been able to find the percentage of the work force working for minimum wages.

How can the average income of the workers of the country be going down at a steady decreasing rate and the average profits of major corporations be rising at an accelerating rate? There is a need for a revolution in that arena.

Where are the Congressmen who will address that issue? Since corporation executives are excused from legitimate taxation and the working class is losing earning power, this translates into less income tax being paid. Can't our legislators see that?

Present congressional leadership is talking 20 to 30 year plans in reducing the deficit. This generation of citizens were the beneficiaries of the deficit and this generation should be held responsible for the elimination of the deficit, or at least a significant decrease in it. The good times can still be had without the embellishment of opulence. We need to practice the frugality people practiced in the early years of the previous century. We need the government to lead the way in this frugality.

We need the strong union movement to reappear. Not so much in wage demands but in cohesion of the work force and to restore a balance to economic and political power. We need the unions to once again bridge the communication chasm that has appeared between management and the work force.

When large profits are made by a company, a thirteen million dollar bonus to an already overpaid executive would be better spent if distributed to the workforce who produced that profit. How can one person spend thirteen million dollars sensibly, let alone a huge salary? This added income was supposed to be used to create jobs, at least that is the propaganda when this type of situation is brought up for legislative review. Our government can close the gap between the rich and their workers. The rich corporations become rich and make huge profits usually with the assistance of our government financing. That statement includes the oil companies which are receiving huge benefits from present legislation.

Suggestions

If we believe our own propaganda about free enterprise then let enterprises such as pharmaceutical companies compete in the market place.

Tax "bonus" payments at a higher rate than contract salary income. This would include any income above the stated salary level of the job.

It seems obvious that indirect taxes rather than direct taxes would be the best avenue for true growth of revenue as well as foster a decrease in tax complaining.

Taxes should never exceed the proven needs of the state.

We have the military capability to destroy any city in the world so there is little need for the huge military budget and expenditures. Congress should get the truth on this subject. Most of the information concerning this is classified in order to withhold the truth rather than for security reasons.

The biggest threat to our social stability is the increasing population. Immigration reform is necessary but this is only a drop-in-the-bucket compared to what really needs to be done. Public emphasis on smaller families is necessary and availability of birth control should be universal. We can no longer afford to take in immigrants with cultural emphasis on large families.

It might be possible to reduce the size of families by eliminating the dependent deduction on the 1040. If we wish to keep the dependent deduction, it might be possible to lower the fertility rate by limiting the deduction to two dependents. Some would argue that this would only increase the request for food stamps and other such benefits. Well, we can also limit food stamp benefits to two dependents. Our increase in population is the most serious problem confronting the country today and in the future. It would be best to eliminate the dependent tax adjustment from the 1040 completely.

A strong justice system is critical to safeguarding individual rights. The courts must be accessible to every citizen, especially including those without financial resources.

The members of the Supreme Court should be liable to recall. They should have term limits, maybe twenty five years. Amend the Constitution.

In January 2010, five justices of the U.S. Supreme Court ruled that corporations have a First Amendment right to spend unlimited funds promoting or attacking candidates in local, state and federal elections. This decision rolls back many years of legal precedent prohibiting direct corporate involvement in elections. The First Amendment was never intended to let nonhuman business corporations spend unlimited corporate cash to influence our elections. Corporations are not people. They do not vote, and they should not be allowed to have such an overwhelming influence on elections. Corporations were already spending considerable amounts of money to influence elections, but the Supreme Court decision permits corporate executives to dip into corporate treasuries and spend as much as they want to buy lawmakers and punish those who stand up for the public interest. To make matters worse, most of this new spending will be hidden from the public. Corporate front groups will sponsor cynical advertisements supporting industry-friendly candidates and attacking public servants who stand up to corporations; the public will not know who is funding the ads.

If corporations want to contribute to a political campaign they should do so through individuals in the corporations and all contributor's names should be available to the public. The Supreme Court decision creates a situation similar to a bushwacker hiding behind a hedge and taking pot-shots at someone coming down the sidewalk. The walker doesn't know where the shot is coming from and who is doing the shooting. There is no protection from the assault and all the walker can do is duck.

Members of Congress should have term limits of perhaps twelve years and their retirement funds should be of such a nature that they would have to obtain other employment once they did retire. A four year Representative should not be eligible for federal retirement income other than social security. It would be possible for a person to spend twelve years in each of the legislative bodies and be eligible for a pension comparable to one in the military.

If members of Congress approach their duty from a negative position and refuse to indulge in meaningful discussion then we have no choice but to get rid of those members who are impeding progress. A petition of recall is in order. If that doesn't work then other means must be employed. Get your placards ready.

It is unfortunate that our government is taking out new loans in order to pay off old loans. If a loan is to be obtained shouldn't there be some idea on where the money will be obtained to pay it off?

This was the end of my discussion but a news story in the *Erie Times-News* on 26 August 2011 indicated an Associated Press GfK poll of Aug 18-22 put public congressional support at twelve percent. Would it be fair to ask, "What do they care?" My association in and with politicos was that you could challenge them face-to-face and your comments would roll from them like water from a duck's back. Criticism made them more belligerent instead of cooperative. Why did the Supreme Court approve unlimited anonymous political contributions? Why isn't that problem being rectified? The people without morals on the Supreme Court outnumber those with morals 5 to 4.

After the first Obama election to the presidency, Senator Mitch McConnell said "our job is to make him a one term president." How the hell could we ever expect to get anything accomplished with that attitude. President Reagan and Tip O'Neill were able to get things done and move the country forward.

It is the duty of all who wish justice to protest against injustice and the most obvious place to start is with discriminatory legislation. When asked why he was in prison, Thoreau asked, "and why are you out there?"

The End

www.ingramcontent.com/pod-product-compliance
Lightning Source LLC
Chambersburg PA
CBHW060626290526
45793CB00001B/164